HOPE IS HERE

A REFLECTIVE BOOK ON RECLAIMING FAITH & HOPE IN THE MIDST OF LIFE'S CHALLENGES

OLINDA DESROSIERS

Copyright © 2025 by Olinda Desrosiers

All rights are reserved, and no part of this publication may be reproduced, distributed, or transmitted in any manner, whether through photocopying, recording, or any other electronic or mechanical methods, without the explicit prior written permission of the publisher. This restriction applies to any form or means of reproduction or distribution.

Exceptions to this rule include brief quotations that may be incorporated into critical reviews, as well as certain other noncommercial uses that are allowed by copyright law. Any such usage must adhere to the specified conditions and permissions outlined by the copyright holder.

Formatted by Hmdpublishing

THE WHY?

I would like to give you the opportunity and confidence to complete and fulfill anything you put your mind to by following a series of tasks. I want you to embrace yourself regardless of your situation. I want you to start speaking affirmations over yourself and your family daily and trust the positivity that you say. Words are powerful. You are not a failure. Whatever negative thoughts or feelings you have about yourself or your situation, you will soon find that you can change that. Use my stories and experiences as an example as you assess yourself using the prompts and questions at the end of each chapter. It's important to dig deep and be honest with yourself so God can use you and provide the instructions you need.

DEDICATION

I dedicate this book to my husband Geno and our five children, Hezron, Hadassah, Zephaniah, Adonijah, and Azriel. You guys have allowed me to become the person that I am today.

ACKNOWLEDGMENT

As I'm writing this book today, I am in awe. I can't believe that this is my first book. I was nervous and still am. I think that this process became an opening to so many other discoveries. I want to thank my friends and family, who constantly encourage me to be a better version of myself each day. I thank God for the strength He has given me to complete this book. Lastly, I would also like to thank my husband. You have shown me that there is so much greatness inside me and more to share with the world. I love you with all my heart.

First and foremost, I want to thank my husband for his unwavering support and for allowing me to share glimpses of our marriage in this book. Your love and encouragement mean the world to me.

A heartfelt thank you to Hezron, who gifted me the title for this book two years ago—your inspiration laid the foundation for this journey.

To Erlande, thank you for your meticulous proofreading, organization, and editing. I deeply appreciate the time and effort you sacrificed to help bring my vision to life on paper.

To my dear friends, Marcha, Veronica, Johnna, and Erica, thank you for standing with me in prayer and offering your unwavering encouragement. Your support has been a source of strength throughout this process.

To everyone who contributed ideas and insights, your input has been invaluable in shaping this book. I apologized if I forgot anybody.

Finally, I extend my gratitude to my church family at Bread of Life International Worship Center. Thank you, Pastor Rudolph, and Latoya Moseley, for giving me the space to spread my wings and step out of my comfort zone. Your faith in me has been a blessing.

This book would not have been possible without each of you. Thank you for being part of this journey.

ABOUT THE AUTHOR

Olinda Desrosiers was raised in Providence, Rhode Island, after her parents immigrated from Saint Martin. She currently resides in Rhode Island with her husband Geno, who she has been married to for 15 years, and their five children: Hezron, Hadassah, Zephaniah, Adonijah, and Azriel. Olinda is a Pastor at Bread of Life International Worship Center (BOLIWC), located in East Providence, RI.

Olinda is a life coach and a mentor to many. Her mission is to pray, encourage and empower women going through difficult times in their lives and relationships. Olinda studied at The University of Rhode Island and received a bachelor's degree in human development and Family Studies in 2008. She has been working in the mental health field since 2006. She enjoys helping families find solutions and hope in their circumstances. It has always been her desire to help and assist families. She currently works in Child and Family Services as a Social Caseworker.

CONTENTS

01. Who am I? 9
02. Discovering My Why 11
03. There is Hope for You! 14
04. What I Needed During Hard Times 20
05. Lessons Learned and Shared 23
06. Embracing Self-Love Inward and Outward Love 26
07. Reflecting on Disappointments & Expectations 30
08. My Upbringing: Reflecting on Cultural Expectations ... 33
09. Reflections on Family Influence 38
10. A Time for Change 42
11. Reflecting on Disappointments and Expectations 47
12. Cultural Expectations 52
13. Reflecting on Duties in Marriage as a Wife 57
14. Transparency 64
15. Being Set Free! Surrendering My Will to God 70
16. Hope Restored 74
17. Motherhood and Raising a Family 80
18. Godly Tips For Kingdom Families 87
19. Pain to Power 92
20. Prayer & Fasting 97
21. Daily Devotions 103
22. Walking In Victory! 105
23. Embracing God's Work In My Life 111

CHAPTER 01

WHO AM I?

I am the eldest of 4. I am a pastor, a wife, and a mother of 5 beautiful children ranging from ages 14 years old to 3 years old. I have been married to my wonderful husband for 15 years and going on forever. I studied at The University of Rhode Island and received a bachelor's degree in human development and Family Studies in 2008. While at the university I began to develop skills to work with women and children. I went on to work in the mental health and social services field and have dedicated myself to it for 16 years. I enjoy helping families find solutions and hope in their circumstances. Together we learned about ourselves and experienced much growth and healing. It's always been a desire to offer inspiration and encouragement to families. Everybody deserves a second chance no matter what. In my profession, I work with children and families and provide them with the support they need to form meaningful relationships and empower them. I'm an outgoing individual who likes to give people the benefit of the doubt. I meet weekly with my friends and mentees and hold them accountable to their goals. We pray together and find solutions to their issues and difficult situations.

REFLECTIVE QUESTIONS

How do you define your life (e.g., family, career, community, purpose)?

_____

_____

_____

_____

What principles from Scripture guide your approach to mentoring and supporting others?

_____

_____

_____

_____

BIBLE VERSES

Galatians 6:9 *"Let us not become weary in doing good, for at the proper time we will reap a harvest if we do not give up."*

Jeremiah 29:11 *"For I know the plans I have for you, declares the Lord, plans to prosper you and not harm you, plans to give you hope and a future."*

CLOSING PRAYER

Dear Heavenly Father, I thank You for the plans You have for me, plans to prosper and not to harm me, to give me hope and a future, as You promised in Jeremiah 29:11. In moments of weariness, remind me of Galatians 6:9—to not grow weary in doing good, for in due season I will reap if I do not give up. Strengthen my heart and renew my faith, trusting that Your timing is perfect. Help me to persevere with hope, knowing that You are guiding my steps. Amen.

CHAPTER 02

DISCOVERING MY WHY

The subject, Hope, is so important to me because there was a point in my life when I felt so hopeless. I felt stuck, like there was no way out. I felt numb like there was nothing that I could do. Yeah, I prayed, but I thought I was missing something. I couldn't put my finger on it. I almost felt ignored by God because it seemed as if He never answered when I called upon His name. During that time, I would encourage others through their own situations, but I didn't know how to uplift myself. I didn't know how to petition and pray for myself and my own needs. I was stuck. Occasionally, the Lord would send people my way to intercede for me and thankfully they provided what I needed during those moments. I had dreams of being great and doing big things but didn't know how to get there. In the Bible, I read how God's servants fulfilled duties for the kingdom of God, received riches, and were used by Him. For example, Abraham, Moses, Joseph: God enlarged their territories, as they served Him. He spoke to them clearly and guided them on the most challenging journeys of their lives. Why couldn't He assist me? I told God, if You can do this for them back then, you can do it for me now. The question was, how was that going to happen. I wanted to be someone who would significantly impact many people's lives. I tried to lean on God as they did wholly, but it felt out of my grasp. Yes, I read scriptures, but I wondered if any of them were for me. Could God truly make a severe impact in my life? I almost questioned if the Lord was accurate in choosing me and making His promises to me when I did not see any change in my life or my family.

REFLECTIVE QUESTIONS

Reflecting on your journey, how have you seen God's provision and intervention in times when you felt stuck or ignored?

_____
_____
_____
_____

What steps have you taken to overcome feelings of doubt and uncertainty about God's Plan for your life and your ability to impact others?

_____
_____
_____
_____

BIBLE VERSES

Isaiah 41:10 *"So do not fear, for I am with you; do not be dismayed, for I am your God. I will strengthen you and help you; I will uphold you with my righteous right hand."*

Matthew 6:25-26 *"Therefore I tell you, do not worry about your life, what you will eat or drink; or about your body, what you will wear. Is not life more than food, and the body more than clothes? Look at the birds of the air; they do not sow or reap or store away in barns, and yet your heavenly Father feeds them. Are you not much more valuable than they?"*

CLOSING PRAYER

Dear Heavenly Father,

In times of uncertainty, I turn to You, seeking Your strength and guidance. I acknowledge the challenges that surround me, but I choose to place my hope in You and Your promises. I trust that You are with me, working in ways I cannot see, turning every trial into an opportunity for growth. Lord, help me as I embark on this journey of reclaiming hope, despite the doubts that try to cloud my vision. Remind me that my worth is not defined by my past struggles but by the purpose You've called me to fulfill. You, Lord, are faithful, You are able, and You are good. I surrender all anxieties to You, May Your peace fill me, and may I live with renewed hope, knowing that through You, all things are possible. In Jesus' name I pray, Amen.

CHAPTER 03

THERE IS HOPE FOR YOU!

There were many tough seasons. Some were harder than others. Those I called friends were no longer available, so I began to feel lonely. When you're in high school and college you never think the friend ships you have will break but people change. You change, they change, and you just don't mess with each other anymore. You get married, they get married, you have kids, they have kids, and locations, careers and paths just change. Whether it's you or them, I found that hard. There were people in my life that I felt I was loyal to, but it began to seem as if they never saw me, or my potential and I had to learn the hard way. I tried so hard to fit into their lives but deep down I knew they didn't accept me. The real me. I spoke to the Lord about it, and he told me to let them go and no longer pursue them. That brought me back to my childhood of feeling and wanting to be accepted. So, I formed new relationships with others but those were also short lived, and I also found that hard. I had to reflect on what I may have done wrong to them. Was it something I said or did? I just didn't know. I had to realize that I can only be me, and you can either like me or hate me. It was a reality I had to face and am still facing today. Sometimes your light can shine too bright for people, so they start pulling away from you. Sometimes they don't understand because they have things that they have not been healed from or choose to ignore.

At first, I was salty and upset but that was wasting too much of my energy. I prayed for their well-being as I did for myself and that was the best I could do at that time. I started to feel this way a year after getting married and having a baby. I was close to my cousins. We hung out a lot together then suddenly, they stopped coming over. I was bothered by this, but I started to think that maybe I may have pushed them away because life had been too hard. I thought I just had to learn to balance everything. I struggled with postpartum depression. I didn't understand it back then, so I never got professional help. Somehow, I found a way to pull myself together. As I sat in church one day, I asked the Lord, is there more for me in this life? I felt so out of place all the time that I believed I was missing something! Is working 9 to 5 all You have for me? There must be more. I felt so incomplete. Yes, I went to college and had a degree, but I didn't feel like I accomplished anything. I was only getting paid minimum wage. I was working several jobs to make ends meet. It was hard. I was not as successful as I imagined. Something was missing. I didn't feel like I made my parents proud. I was the oldest after all and didn't feel like I had set a great example for my younger siblings. Granted I was the first to graduate from college, but what else did I have to offer? I prayed and asked the Lord to show me and guide me.

I believed some things He showed me, but I feared the unknown. I felt like something in me needed to be let loose. After going to a conference in 2017 I found what I had been searching for! I attended a "Reset" Conference in Boston, Massachusetts, that opened my mind to many possibilities for my future. That was the year that I completely and wholeheartedly gave my life to God and truly served Him. I understood Him and the purpose He had for me. I didn't think He thought of me. I was shocked and I felt loved like never before from Jesus Christ. People started to speak over my life, my future, and my situation. This was something new to me and nothing I had ever experienced at my current church. The feelings that I had inside all started to make sense. There was so much more out there than I could have ever imagined. I had to put my faith to the test; there were things done and spoken in that conference that I never imagined I would do in my life. There were new things I witnessed. One example was trusting God to speak through me and to prophesy to others. What an amazing yet slightly terrifying experience that was. It was scary because I wasn't used to talking to others in such a way. It was uncomfortable for me to operate like that for the first time, but it was also very exciting to trust God in this new area of my life. People spoke things over my life that I couldn't fathom.

After this conference, when I read the Word, scriptures finally really began to make sense to me. God was revealing Himself through His Word. He was speaking to me. He illuminated everything on each page just for me to understand. I began to look at my life and decisions differently. I began to dream and imagine the impossible for my life and that things could and would turn around. I chose this topic of reclaiming hope because I want people to know that there is hope and a way out in every situation. There is never a dead-end in life. When I see people in pain or struggling through challenges, I have a burning desire to help or come up with a solution. Even if my world is falling apart, I want to be a pillar of hope, a light or sunshine in someone's life. My hope comes from the Lord. He has helped and guided me in some very dark times in my life. He still is and forever will. When people look at me, they see me laugh and smile but don't see that I have been through a lot of pain. I smile and encourage others because it helps brighten their day and sometimes it encourages me too.

My presence is so strong and captivating that coming in sad and with a heavy heart may make some people feel uncomfortable, so I've faked it until I made it a lot of times. You would only be able to see the truth with the Holy Spirit. That's why it's so important to have a relationship with Him so He can open your spiritual eyes and lead you down the path of righteousness and peace. Although that path may not be easy, there are things you must be delivered from and people that you will have to forgive and potentially let go. I had to learn forgiveness if I wanted to truly begin to reclaim my life and walk in His fullness. Forgiveness isn't for you; it is for God. If we are holding on to unforgiveness and bitterness in our hearts God can't move because it's a blockage. In Matthew 5:8 it says, *"Blessed are the pure in heart for they shall see God"*. Meaning a clean heart and mind is the only way He can truly manifest in your heart. In 1 Peter 5:7 *"Cast all your anxiety on Him because He cares for us"*. Just throw it on Him and let Him carry your burdens. Vengeance is God's only; He knows how to deal with those who have hurt us or caused us any trauma or harm. Romans 12:19 says *"Beloved, never avenge yourselves, but leave it to the wrath of God, for it is written, Vengeance is mine, I will repay, says the Lord."* Even when we may not understand, let Him do it! In the end, it all becomes worth it.

REFLECTIVE QUESTIONS

How has your understanding of God's faithfulness grown through challenging seasons in your life?

_____
_____
_____
_____

In what ways have you been able to share the hope and encouragement you've received with others in similar situations?

_____
_____
_____
_____

What steps can you take to deepen your relationship with God and continue to align with His purposes for your life?

_____
_____
_____
_____

BIBLE VERSES

Isaiah 43:19 *"See, I am doing a new thing! Now it springs up; do you not perceive it? I am making a way in the wilderness and streams in the wasteland."*

Romans 15:13 *"May the God of hope fill you with all joy and peace as you trust in Him, so that you may overflow with hope by the power of the Holy Spirit."*

CLOSING PRAYER

Dear Heavenly Father,

We come before You with hearts full of gratitude, even amid life's storms. In those dark and uncertain times, we often feel misunderstood, dismissed, and distant from the world around us. But we thank You, Lord, for being our constant source of comfort, even when we don't fully understand Your ways. Thank You for surrounding us with family, friends, and a church community to lift us in prayer when we feel lost.

We confess that there were moments when we questioned our purpose and even Your love for us. We cried out in confusion, wondering why we feel so different, so sensitive to the world around us. But, Lord, even when we felt alone and questioned who we were, You never left our side. You gave us a peace that surpassed our understanding, and for that, we are eternally grateful.

Thank You for sending messengers to remind us that You hear our cries, even in Your silence. We are learning to trust in Your plan, knowing that You are working all things for our good. Help us to hold on to that trust, especially when we cannot see the path ahead. May we continue to seek Your guidance, knowing that You are molding us into who You've called us to be.

We ask that You fill our hearts with hope and strengthen our faith, so that we may continue to walk in Your light, knowing that You are always with us. In Your perfect love and timing, we find peace.

In Jesus' name we pray, Amen.

CHAPTER 04

WHAT I NEEDED DURING HARD TIMES

In those dark times in my life, I needed support from my family, church, and friends to pray through it all. I had felt misunderstood and indifferent. I know they didn't get me, some still don't. I didn't learn until later that they don't always have to. What I needed was patience, attention, and support, not validation. There were times when I spoke of things, and people dismissed them. I shed many tears, confused about my purpose on earth. I asked Him a series of questions. Why am I here, Lord? Who do you want me to become? Why am I so sensitive and feel so different about people? At one point I asked God if he hated me. I felt so unaccepted. It felt like people looked at me as if I was crazy. I started to question who I was. But somehow God gave me a sense of peace in many circumstances without me fully understanding. Times when I felt He didn't hear me He would always send me a messenger. That gave some reassurance. I started to trust the Lord and realized that He is still working things for my good, even in His silence.

REFLECTIVE QUESTIONS

Reflecting on moments when you felt misunderstood, how did these experiences shape your trust in God's understanding of your heart?

_____
_____
_____
_____

In what ways has trusting God through difficult times brought you peace and reassurance?

_____
_____
_____
_____

BIBLE VERSES

>**Psalm 34:17** *"The righteous cry out, and the Lord hears them; He delivers them from all their troubles."*
>
>**Isaiah 55:8-9** *"For My thoughts are not your thoughts, neither are your ways My ways, declares the Lord. As the heavens are higher than the earth, so are My ways higher than your ways and My thoughts than your thoughts."*

CLOSING PRAYER

Dear Heavenly Father,

We come before You with hearts full of gratitude, even during life's storms. In those dark and uncertain times, we often feel misunderstood, dismissed, and distant from the world around us. But we thank You, Lord, for being our constant source of comfort, even when we don't fully understand Your ways. Thank You for surrounding us with family, friends, and a church community to lift us in prayer when we felt lost. We confess that there were moments when we questioned our purpose and even Your love for us. We cried out in confusion, wondering why we felt so different, so sensitive to the world around us. But, Lord, even when we felt alone and questioned who we were, you never left our side. You gave us a peace that surpassed our understanding, and for that, we are eternally grateful.

Thank You for sending messengers to remind us that You hear our cries, even in Your silence. We are learning to trust in Your plan, knowing that You are working all things for our good. Help us to hold on to that trust, especially when we cannot see the path ahead. May we continue to seek Your guidance, knowing that You are molding us into who You've called us to be. We ask that You fill our hearts with hope and strengthen our faith, so that we may continue to walk in Your light, knowing that You are always with us. In Your perfect love and timing, we find peace. In Jesus' name I pray, Amen.

CHAPTER 05

LESSONS LEARNED AND SHARED

I have learned that in life, nothing comes easy. At first, I fought by complaining and talking. Don't get me wrong, I am not perfect, and at times I do lose myself when I start to get wrapped up in my feelings and emotions. But I soon realized that fighting also meant working through prayer aloud and in the spirit. I focused more on renouncing things over my life and declared and decreed things over myself and my mind. I had to take charge and authority over my situation (Genesis 1:8). God has given us this gift of prayer. Most of the time we are afraid to use it due to lack of faith in God, ourselves, or our current situations.

There will be struggles, heartache, and hard times in this life, but we have to persevere through it all. I had to. I had to push myself because I wanted a different life and future for myself and my family. I travailed in prayer. Travailing in prayer is that deep prayer where you're crying and wailing to the Lord. You may feel a physical reaction or connection. It is where I felt the most vulnerable and the most connected with Christ. My prayers were coming out of my belly. In this form of prayer, the Holy Spirit takes control over your words. That's when I found peace. God was praying on my behalf. Everything from deep within that I couldn't put in my own words, He knew what they were. God gave me peace that truly surpassed all understanding. I desire to share tips with women and show them a way out because I'm making it out. You must let the Lord in to gain that ability. You must let go of fear and worry and just allow him to lead you.

REFLECTIVE QUESTIONS

In what ways has prayer been transformative in your life, especially during times of vulnerability?

_____

_____

_____

_____

What steps can you take to empower others to lean on God's peace and guidance in their own challenges?

_____

_____

_____

_____

How can you strengthen your faith in God's ability to lead and provide, especially when facing fear and uncertainty?

_____

_____

_____

_____

BIBLE VERSES

Philippians 4:6-7 *"Do not be anxious about anything, but in everything by prayer and supplication with thanksgiving let your requests be made known to God. And the peace of God, which surpasses all understanding, will guard your hearts and your minds in Christ Jesus."*

Roman 5:3-4 *"Not only so, but we also glory in our sufferings, because we know that suffering produces perseverance; perseverance, character; and character, hope."*

James 1:2-4 *"Consider it pure joy, my brothers and sisters, whenever you face trials of many kinds, because you know that the testing of your faith produces perseverance. Let perseverance finish its work so that you may be mature and complete, not lacking anything."*

CLOSING PRAYER

Dear Heavenly Father,

Thank You for the lesson You have taught me through both joy and struggle. I am grateful for every experience that has shaped, whether good or bad, and for the wisdom You have revealed to me along the way. Help me to always see Your hand at work in every circumstance. May I not just learn for myself, but help me to share these lessons with others, offering the comfort and hope that comes from knowing you, despite my own fear and discomfort. Lord, I pray that I never underestimate the power of prayer. Teach me to pray more deeply, more sincerely, and more consistently, understanding that through it I will be drawn to You. As I grow in understanding You and Your will for my life, I ask that You strengthen my faith and help me trust You fully. When uncertainty arises, help me to look to You for reassurance. May my life reflect the benefits of prayer. In Jesus' name I pray, Amen.

CHAPTER 06

EMBRACING SELF-LOVE INWARD AND OUTWARD LOVE

I have struggled with my image since I was a child. Family members always told me I was overweight and needed to stop eating, but they were the ones who fed me. I distinctly remember their words at the young age of nine years old. I was bullied because of my appearance in school and even at church. There was a time when I had lost a tremendous amount of weight in a month. But instead of a compliment, someone at church told me, "You're lucky you're pretty." It's crazy how people have no decorum for the feelings of others and would blatantly make a random comment like that. I know she may have meant well, but her delivery was awful. I questioned myself a lot (*I still struggle with this*). I often feel I need validation but I'm still a work in progress. Unresolved circumstances and traumas follow you into adulthood. But you must take a stand for yourself and against the enemy and push!

For a long time, it felt like I couldn't fit in anywhere or I do anything right! I didn't like who I was and I didn't like others saw me. I wasn't popular or noticed. Outside my home, I was usually funny and outgoing, but I felt like a prisoner. I didn't smile much or laugh. I didn't have any confidence in myself or thought I could accomplish anything significant! People would compliment me on things, and instead of accepting it, I questioned why. My parents at times would compare me to my cousins and friends at church. I felt so inadequate. I would often ask myself why they always said that? Did they value them than me? I longed to be perfect and better for them. I was not taught how to love myself, in fact, I hated my body and my physical appearance. I still wear a cardigan to this day if I don't feel fully comfortable in an outfit. To this day I have to constantly remind myself that I am fearfully and wonderfully made. When I look in the mirror that is what I say to encourage and love myself whenever those negative feelings start returning.

REFLECTIVE QUESTIONS

When did you stop loving yourself?

_____

_____

_____

_____

Read 1 Corinthians 13. How can you speak this chapter over yourself?

_____

_____

_____

_____

In what ways have past experiences shaped the way you view yourself today? Would you like to challenge yourself and think more positively about yourself?

_____

_____

_____

_____

How do you currently seek validation or approval from others? What steps can you take to find inner validation and self-acceptance?

_____

_____

What can you do each day to remind yourself that you are fearfully and wonderfully made, even when feelings of inadequacy arise?

BIBLE VERSE

1 Corinthians 13:4-7 *"4 Love is patient and kind. Love is not jealous or boastful or proud or rude. It does not demand its own way. It is not irritable, and it keeps no record of being wronged. It does not rejoice about injustice but rejoices whenever the truth wins out. Love never gives up, never loses faith, is always hopeful, and endures through every circumstance."*

CLOSING PRAYER:

I praise You Lord because I am fearfully and wonderfully made; Your works are wonderful; I know that full well. My frame was not hidden from You when I was made in the secret place, when I was woven together in the depths of the earth. I am worthy, I am enough. I love myself, thoroughly. I embrace my flaws. I celebrate my strengths. I am beautiful, no matter my length or width. I cherish my heart; I honor my soul. I am whole, I am complete, and my love for myself makes me whole. In Jesus' name I pray, Amen.

CHAPTER 07

REFLECTING ON DISAPPOINTMENTS & EXPECTATIONS

For a long time, I saw myself as overweight, a victim of molestation, ugly, broken, sad, lacking confidence, low self-esteem, and someone who wasn't taken seriously. I wanted to be free of these thoughts. I felt unaccomplished. I felt stuck like I may never see any change. I hated going out and getting dressed. I analyzed everything that I wore. I didn't like seeing my love handles through my clothes, so I always wore a cardigan to cover that up (I still do). Of course, I didn't think I was pretty because I wasn't told I was. I lacked confidence in myself because I always struggled in school. I was always compared to how well my cousins did in school. Frankly, it was so annoying. I was also envious of my younger siblings because they did so well in school, and it didn't seem difficult for them. They spoke well. When they accomplished things, they were often praised and recognized. I had a lot of things in my mind that didn't make sense. Instead of speaking of them out loud I chose to stay quiet. I stayed quiet for years. I couldn't put into words what I saw and felt. I asked God to change my perspective of myself. I asked God to clear out my eyes so I could begin to *SEE* myself as He saw me. I didn't want to only see myself through others compliments on things I did. I wanted to see value and praise in myself for me, instead of always comparing myself and trying to act like others. I always compare myself and try to act like others. That was not a good fit for me. I felt like a fraud. I knew the only person I had to be was myself.

REFLECTIVE QUESTIONS

What do you love and appreciate about yourself at this moment?

_____
_____
_____
_____

How can you be kinder today both in your thoughts and actions towards yourself?

_____
_____
_____
_____

What are some ways you have dealt with disappointments, that resulted in you feeling worse about yourself?

_____
_____
_____
_____

BIBLE VERSES

Psalms 139 *"For You formed my inward parts; You knitted me together in my mother's womb. I praise You, for I am fearfully and wonderfully made. Wonderful are Your works; my soul knows it very well."*

> **1 Corinthians 6:19-20** *"Do you not know that your bodies are temples of the Holy Spirit, who is in you, whom you have received from God? You are not your own; you were bought at a price. Therefore, honor God with your bodies."*

CLOSING PRAYER

Heavenly Father, You know my beginning and my end. I trust in Your perfect plan, knowing that You will make a way even when I cannot see one. When doubt creeps in, remind me that I am fearfully and wonderfully made in Your image, crafted with purpose. Help me to rest in the assurance of Your love and guidance. In Jesus' name I pray, Amen.

CHAPTER 08

MY UPBRINGING: REFLECTING ON CULTURAL EXPECTATIONS

REFLECTING ON CULTURAL EXPECTATIONS

There were not many compliments growing up. Any child would want validation on different aspects of their lives because it can add to self-worth. If I had an issue, no one really sat down to talk to me calmly. It was always "well what's wrong with you" but it was asked in a way that turned me off from expressing how I truly felt. My feelings were often hurt, I was frustrated, I felt like a burden, so I would make up conclusions in my head. Now that I am older and much more observant, I've grown to understand them more and I can't blame my parents for the way they treated me because they didn't know any better.

Growing up for them was rough. My mother had a very strict upbringing, so she was a lot more reserved. She was the second oldest and had many responsibilities as a woman and caregiver. She had to do well in school, cook, clean, and help with the house. When her work was not done well, she was disciplined harshly. She was not raised in an openly affectionate home, so she raised me based on her own experiences and what she knew. Hearing the words "I Love You" were foreign to me. Although she didn't express her love with heartfelt words, she expressed love in her own way. She always made sure we had food to eat, we were dressed well, and well taken care of. She didn't treat either of us differently. She encouraged us to be strong, independent, and not to take smack from anyone. In our youth it seemed very demanding, but as an adult, I value the lessons she instilled in us. She has a very big heart and has been known to be very caring and supportive of others. I recall being 12 or 13 years old, having so many pimples on my face, and hating how I looked. I remember telling my mother that I wanted to kill myself. My mother didn't tell me she loved me or how beautiful I was or to love myself as I was and that we grow in beauty. She didn't tell me this was part of puberty and that these pimples would pass. Instead, she made every effort to buy creams and lotions to help me feel good about myself, but I still struggled with my image. I just couldn't see myself as beautiful. When people would say I was pretty, I wondered who they were speaking to.

My dad was raised by a family that showed him lots of love and affection. His mother was much older and couldn't take care of him after his father died. Although he didn't fully grow up with his mother, he was very close to her and continued to have a relationship with her. We would often go to Haiti to visit her and other members of our family. My dad always tried, but he usually talked at me, rather than to me. He was the most verbal one when expressing himself. He often told us when he was proud of us. He would spend time with us and teach us to study the bible, read the Haitian Christian song books, and play games during outings. He would show affection through jokes, rubbing of the head, a hug or a handshake. My dad did this to all my friends when they came to the house even if he didn't know them. As a result of their rougher upbringing in Haiti and through the belief that America was the land of opportunity, at their core, my parents believed in creating a better life for their children. They believed they could express their love and support by making sure our lives were easier than theirs. The best way they knew how to do that was by encouraging us to go to church, do well in school, complete our education, and be good people.

Believe it or not, everything seemed like it was a competition. It was me against the world and I wasn't meant to succeed in anything. I wasn't successful the way I imagined I would be at my young age. I was a first generational person in my family to go to college and graduate, but I saw others around me living well and appearing successful. I thought there was something wrong with me and felt was stuck. The thoughts in my head never made sense when I spoke. When I went to conferences and heard about people's testimonies, I told myself I had so much catching up to do. But how? How was I going to get there? I had to reflect on my life and myself a lot. What I realized was I didn't believe in Linda. My words did not align with how I felt inside so I had to change my thinking.

REFLECTIVE QUESTIONS

What cultural or familial expectations have influenced your decisions and actions?

_____
_____
_____
_____

How have they impacted your sense of identity and purpose?

_____
_____
_____
_____

What messages about self-love did you receive growing up, and how have those words influenced your beliefs about yourself?

_____
_____
_____
_____

BIBLE VERSE

1 John 4:7-8 *"Beloved, let us love one another, for love is from God, and whoever loves has been born of God and knows God. Anyone who does not love, does not know God, because God is love."*

Ephesians 4:29 *"Let no corrupting talk come out of your mouths, but only such as is good for building up, as fits the occasion, that it may give grace to those who hear."*

DECLARATION:

I'm a child of God and a new creation. I was born to succeed and have the abundant life. I will not back down because of my past or circumstances. I am resilient, I am victorious in all I do. Everything I do and touch is blessed in the name of Jesus. I favor God and His grace. In Jesus' name I pray, Amen.

INSERT SELF PORTRAIT

What do you see? What do you want to say to yourself? Only list positive words

_____, _____, _____, _____, _____

CHAPTER 09

REFLECTIONS ON FAMILY INFLUENCE

I felt like there was so much overwhelming pressure on me to be perfect and be on top of everything. When something was not completed well or right or to standard, I felt like I let my family down. Everyone called and relied on me for everything. I was always asked by my aunts and uncles to go speak to my cousins if there was a crisis happening. My siblings didn't really like me. It was always three against 1. My parents worked a lot, and I was always left to babysit them. I had to cook and maintain the home. It was exhausting. I believe that's why I struggled to be happy at home because I had to be an adult at such a young age. I felt I had to accomplish things and be a good example. The pressure was on. I was the first to go to college in my family and the first to marry. I tried my best to stay strong around my siblings and let them know that they could count on me whenever they needed me. I had a special connection with each of my siblings. I knew when something was wrong with each of them. Each of my siblings are unique in their own way. They were so bright and could pick up on anything they put their minds to. I so envied that. Their vocabulary and intellect are remarkable. I wanted to be like them. They did well in college and passed with honors while I struggled. I looked so down on myself and felt that I could not offer anything to them because I wasn't like them. My brothers loved breaking things apart and putting them together. Today they are both successful engineers. I'm genuinely inspired by how far they've come. They are always learning new material to better equip themselves in their professions. My sister read a lot which explains why her words and vocabulary were so fascinating. I'm so proud of her. She enrolled in the National Guard and received a bachelor's degree in Radiologic Technology. She was the first to go into the military. She took risks. I envied that in her, too, because I never did anything crazy or spontaneous in my life. My sister is a great seamstress among other things and does well in everything she does.

When I look at my life. It seems like I lived for people and didn't get to enjoy things in life as much as I would have liked for myself. I'm the oldest of 4, so I wanted to provide for my younger siblings, but they were the ones assisting me. There was a time in my life when I really struggled. I was afraid to tell them, and my pride had the best of me, but I knew that they were the only ones that I could count on. Although I felt so much shame and guilt, I felt genuinely grateful for their help. I'm forever grateful to have been blessed with such beautiful siblings, Rudny, Erlande, and Steven. They never intentionally let me feel less than in any kind of way. The thoughts in my head and how I perceived myself caused the guilt. My desire is that they will always know they can call and rely on me for whatever they may need.

REFLECTIVE QUESTIONS

Did you have siblings, cousins, or children around you growing up? How did they affect the way you saw yourself?

_____
_____
_____
_____

Name one person who impacted who you are today and why?

_____
_____
_____
_____

BIBLE VERSES

Psalm 20:7 *"Some trust in chariots and some in horses, but we trust in the name of the Lord our God."*

Isaiah 2:22 *"Stop trusting in mere humans, who have but a breath in their nostrils. Why hold them in esteem?"*

CLOSING PRAYER:

Dear heavenly Father,

I come before You with a heart full of gratitude for the gift of family. Thank You for the guidance, wisdom, and love that my family has poured into me. I recognize the profound impact they have had on shaping who I am, and I appreciate every moment of instruction, every word of encouragement, and every act of love that *helped nurture my soul. Lord, I am thankful for the values, the faith, and the example that my family has imparted onto me. I also acknowledge that, at times, there may have been negative influences or teachings that could have blocked me from receiving the truth of Your Word. Father, I ask for Your forgiveness for any hurt or confusion these may have caused in my life. Though people may influence my thoughts, my decisions, and my actions, I know that Your Word is the ultimate guide. Help me to rely on Your strength and wisdom, not on the fleeting promises of men. Teach me to put my faith in You, trusting that Your plan for my life is greater than anything I can ever imagine. Lord, I pray for healing where there has been hurt, clarity where there has been confusion, and strength to move forward in faith. Thank You for Your unconditional love and for Your faithful provision. In Jesus' name I pray, Amen.*

CHAPTER 10

A TIME FOR CHANGE

I don't remember specifically when my mindset and thoughts started to change but I know it wasn't overnight. I had to take baby steps. Reading the Word of God and asking the Lord to provide illumination and revelation through the scriptures is what helped me change how I viewed myself. Connecting with people that may have experienced what I was going through also helped me greatly. I often spoke to myself in the mirror and talked through my issues aloud instead of bottling them up inside. I felt like I was going crazy if I didn't let these feelings out. I started looking at verses on the subject I was dealing with. I put them on flashcards and posted some of them on my wall. I would say the scriptures aloud and add myself or my name so I could speak life to my situation. I looked for sermons and inspirational sessions on the web that could help me change my thinking. These things sometimes worked, but it always led me to speak to my Father. He was the only one who understood me and knew what I was battling.

One day while I was in meditation, I had an epiphany. All my life I made plans trusting that God was going to come through. The one thing I never asked Him is whether He agreed with these goals I made for myself. He showed me a vision of my future regarding my kids and other goals I had set for myself. Right then and there, I was like; I got this all wrong. The verse for me that year was Proverbs 3:5-6 which reads, *"Trust in the Lord with all your heart and lean not on your understanding. In all your ways submit to Him, and He will make your paths straight."* Right then, I started asking the Lord for direction on everything, even on what I should wear or what route I should take home from work and waited for His response. Some people asked how you can hear from God. I told them that it's about staying quiet and being open to receiving what He wants to say to you. There were times that what He asked me to do felt uncomfortable, but I had to be obedient. At times the Lord spoke through my children, the radio, a verse, or people. Sometimes He will put a thought in your mind that encourages you to make the next move.

REFLECTIVE QUESTIONS

What has changed to make you feel the way that you do about yourself now? Writing is so important; you will get your breakthrough by doing so!

_____
_____
_____
_____

What can you do differently as you reflect on your life and/or circumstances?

_____
_____
_____
_____

What words can you speak to yourself to provide you with the courage you need?

_____
_____
_____
_____

Now, when you look at yourself, what do you see?

_____
_____

_____

_____

Write a letter to yourself, offering words of encouragement and affirmation. What empowering messages would you like to hear to strengthen your resolve and self-confidence?

Dear Self, _____

_____
_____
_____
_____
_____
_____
_____
_____
_____
_____
_____
_____
_____
_____
_____
_____
_____
_____
_____
_____
_____
_____

CLOSING PRAYER

Heavenly Father, I come before You with a heart of gratitude and humility. I thank You for how far You have brought me, even when I didn't realize how my mindset was shifting. Thank You for the baby steps that led me closer to understanding who I am in You. Lord, I ask that You continue to reveal Your truth to me through Your Word and guide me in every step I take.

I acknowledge that in the past, I trusted in my own plans, but now I surrender everything to You. I declare Proverbs 3:5-6 over my life: "I will trust in You with all my heart and lean not on my own understanding. I will submit my ways to You, and I trust that You will make my paths straight."

Thank You for being my constant source of understanding, for hearing me when I felt no one else could. I commit to seeking Your direction in every aspect of my life, even in the smallest decisions. Help me to stay quiet and listen for Your voice, whether it comes through scripture, others, or the still small voice within.

Give me the courage to be obedient, even when it feels uncomfortable, and remind me that You are always with me. Thank You for speaking to me in ways that only I can understand, and for leading me to the future You have prepared for me. In Jesus' name I pray, Amen.

CHAPTER 11

REFLECTING ON DISAPPOINTMENTS AND EXPECTATIONS

I have been afraid of not fitting in my whole life. I lacked confidence in myself. I worried that whatever I did would not come out well. When I had an idea of something, it always changed when someone said something about it. I was intimidated by people's opinions of me. To them, my words didn't make sense, so I asked myself, "why share"? Although not everyone told me how they felt about me, at times I could sense it. No matter how hard I worked, no one saw my true potential, not at home, school, church, or even at my jobs. I decided that all the work and energy I put into everything else was the same amount I should be putting into Christ.

There were a lot of disappointments. People I trusted and confided in hurt me. Friends I thought would always be there, disappeared and stopped returning my calls. Friends and family seemed fake when they spoke to me. I could sense there was something off, but I never said a thing. I had a lot of insecurities for fear of being rejected. Through all of that, I remained true to myself, never tried to be different, and I was sincere and kind to everyone. I knew I had to bring my issues and concerns to the Lord and He gave me the answers which brought understanding. It was a sad time because I'm usually encouraged when I speak to people, but no one was around. When I spoke to the Lord about my concerns, He answered saying that they were going through their own issues and the best thing to do at the moment was to pray for them, so I did. I realized that there are people who are only placed in my life for a season, a reason, or a lifetime, but once my assignment is completed, their time is up. My advice for anyone who has experienced much loss in friendships or relationships is to try to remember the situation or season during that loss. Ask God to reveal what type of situation you both were in and what the purpose was for them being in your life, if there was one. Let go and let the Lord lead the rest of the way for you instead of holding on and being bitter. He will send new people in to your circle.

I can recall a specific time in my life where the feeling of rejection was heavy on me. I just knew I had disappointed my family. I was working in my field as a case worker full-time and as a certified nursing assistant part-time. I thought I would be making it rain with lots of money but that wasn't the case. I had bills to pay, and the extra income wasn't always enough. My parents always encouraged us to go to college and get a degree, but this degree I chose didn't provide the income I expected. Both of my parents were born and raised in Haiti. They came to America in their mid-30s in hopes that their children would make better decisions and live a better life than them. But here I was, working at the same nursing home as my father, doing the same kind of work, and making the same minimum wage. He had to be disappointed. Working as a CNA was not what they had in mind for my future, even though I worked full-time at a mental health agency that coincided with my major in college. Even though I was doing my best to stay on the right path and do the right things, pay bills, take care of my duties, my siblings, and my responsibilities at church.

I was hurt to find out that no matter how hard I tried they were not satisfied. To them, through the lenses of the American dream, this was not success, happiness or comfort. They knew there was a better life for me out there, and they didn't want to see me struggling so hard. They just didn't know how to properly communicate that although they were not satisfied with how hard life had become for me, they still supported me and loved me through it all and would provide any assistance when needed. My mother even encouraged me to go back to school to get my master's degree. She offered to help me financially and thought a more accomplished degree would provide better opportunities for higher pay. But I was not interested because college was a challenge for me. I struggled so much in and did not want to be put myself through that again. If God had that in His plans for my life, then I would not have dismissed the idea so quickly

REFLECTIVE QUESTIONS

Who or what in your life or past has caused you to feel rejected? What was the outcome? Reflect on instances where rejection has affected you deeply. How did these experiences shape your self-perception and relationship?

_____
_____
_____
_____

Reflecting on disappointments, how have you sought healing and reconciliation?

_____
_____
_____
_____

How does rejection affect your self-esteem and confidence?

_____
_____
_____
_____

How has your past experiences of rejection shaped your current beliefs and behaviors?

_____
_____

How can you turn rejection into motivation for personal growth and improvement?

BIBLE VERSES

2 Corinthians 1:3-4 *"Receive comfort when you're overcoming rejection so that you can comfort others."*

Psalms 34:17-20 *"The Lord is close to the broken hearted and saves those who are crushed in spirit. The righteous person may have many troubles, but the Lord delivers him from them all, he protects all his bones, not one of them will be broken."*

CLOSING PRAYER

Father, You say in Your word that I will receive Your comfort when I'm overcoming rejection. I will receive Your comfort. I trust in Your faithfulness to heal my wounds and restore my spirit. Help me to embrace Your comfort so that I may, in turn, offer it to others who are hurting. Thank You for Your unending love and grace, which sustains me through every trial. In Jesus' name I pray, Amen.

CHAPTER 12

CULTURAL EXPECTATIONS

Growing up in a Haitian household, cultural expectations weighed heavily on my shoulders. I was told that the child must make do better than the parent. Both of my parents did very well in school and because they grew up in poor households and didn't have the opportunity to attend college themselves, they emphasized the importance of education, careers, and success. When I became the first in my family to graduate from college, it was a momentous occasion filled with pride and celebration. However, the path to this achievement was full of challenges and internal struggles. All Haitians know the main desires of the parents is for their children to go to college, make something of their life, and get married, all while serving God. But we were only encouraged to become a nurse, a doctor, or a lawyer. That's where they thought stability, money, and comfort was, as if there was no success in anything else. The dream my parents expected us to live was difficult. As the oldest, I felt I couldn't let them down.

I didn't know it then but what I was subjecting myself through at that time was family-pleasing, just constantly trying to appease my family at the expense of my own wants, needs, and comfort. I started my degree in nursing because that's what my parents wanted for me even though I struggled. It made me depressed to the point I wanted to end it all. All my friends were passing with flying colors, while I was failing badly no matter how hard I tried. I stayed in nursing because that's what my parents expected. Everyone struggles, just keep working hard and suck it up cause life isn't easy, but you'll get to where you need to be eventually. My parents didn't understand when people said, "college isn't for me." To them, what other choice did you have? My parents worked hard to put all 4 of us through college. So, when I got my Bachelors' Degree, it was a joy to the family and a huge milestone. They didn't understand that you shouldn't push people into a major just because you think it's best. Not everyone has the interest, skill, capacity, or ability to pursue a path that doesn't truly fit them. They weren't aware of the many opportunities and majors that could also bring stability and joy.

When my mother asked if I would get my master's after I graduated, I told her I would think about it. I don't think you understand how much I was struggling in college I didn't want to return to that pain and feel less of myself, especially while starting my own family. I knew my mom meant well because she saw I wasn't getting paid what she had expected with an College degree. I think at that time, Haitians believed a college degree meant more money. She wanted me to live comfortably and not struggle financially. But I felt I disappointed her because I wasn't where I would like to have been financially either. I also did not want to pursue a master's degree when I didn't think I could do well enough to even get a bachelor's degree. So again, I started to pray and ask God what He had planned for my future.

I still had the desire to help people and I wanted to make my family proud, just not to the extent of me not feeling free. I had to do something different. I explored different avenues that would give me the opportunity to make more income. After meeting with a leader from church she talked about social work. I told her it was not something I was really interested in but after that chat I met with my school advisor a couple of days later and changed my major to Human Development and Family Studies. Right then and there it was as if a burden was lifted off. I was no longer carrying that weight. My thinking was clearer, and I was passing with flying colors. The only downfall was the number of papers I had to type. I progressed better yearly. I enjoyed all my classes and loved what I was learning. It came naturally. I realized then that I was finally beginning to live for me, and I finally felt free.

Each year I started to write down goals. The Bible says in Habakkuk 2:2-3 (ESV) *"And the Lord answered me, "Write the vision; make it plain on the tablets, so he may run who reads it. For still the vision awaits its appointed time; it hastens to end-it will not lie. If it seems slow, wait for it; it will surely come; it will not delay."* This scripture gave me life. The reason why things were not happening was that I wasn't writing them down. It's like writing a contract between yourself and God, once it's completed, you check it off. When I write things down, I put the date so that I can testify how great God is when He, in turn, provides completion. My goal is to accomplish something new each year. In this season I have been completing a task every month. Here I am writing a book, with my 3-month-old in one hand. This was always in the back of my head but never thought I was going to do it. Guess what though, I wrote it down. I didn't feel qualified, and I was intimidated by others when I started to write my book because I thought they were more established than I. I didn't even know where to begin, but God moved and made provision. God provided a vision in prayer, and I completed it. There is nothing too hard for GOD!

REFLECTIVE QUESTION

How has prayer or spiritual guidance helped you navigate through moments of uncertainty or conflicting expectations? Share examples of how prayer or seeking spiritual guidance has provided clarity and direction in challenging times.

_____

_____

_____

_____

BIBLICAL VERSE

Habakkuk 2:2-3 *"And the Lord answered me: 'Write the vision; make it plain on tablets, so he may run who reads it. For still the vision awaits its appointed time; it hastens to the end—it will not lie. If it seems slow, wait for it; it will surely come; it will not delay.'"*

REFLECTION AND GOAL SETTING

Reflect on the cultural and familial expectations that have shaped your journey and recognize the importance of aligning your goals with personal aspirations and God's guidance. Setting clear goals and seeking divine wisdom has been pivotal in navigating through uncertainties and finding fulfillment in many endeavors.

GOAL SETTING

(Let's start small. Set 3-5 goals you want to complete in the next MONTH, 6 MONTHS, or YEAR):

1. _____
2. _____

3. _____
4. _____
5. _____

Starting Point. *(Choose one goal above and lets begin to actively work towards it. Please feel free to use a notebook to document your goals, steps, process, scriptures, words of affirmation, and whatever else you need to help encourage you through the goal. Let's start with your first step and how you plan to complete it)*:

I will... _____

_____

_____

_____

_____

Remember, the plan is to start and then we can work on maintaining and consistency!

Verses to Back Up Goal (s) Write them here:

CHAPTER 13

REFLECTING ON DUTIES IN MARRIAGE AS A WIFE

Marriage is hard. Marriage is a blessing, but it is also warfare. It's a journey filled with challenges that test not only our love for each other but also our faith in God's plan for our union. The enemy constantly seeks to undermine marriages, stirring up conflicts over trivial matters and planting seeds of doubt about our choices. Many times, I've found myself questioning if I made the right decision in marrying my husband. It's so challenging to coexist with another person. At times you forget about yourself and your own needs. Living with someone from a different background and with different struggles can be overwhelming. There were moments when I've felt the urge to run away and escape the pressures that came with marriage. But would I accomplish anything by doing that? NO! But I've come to realize that these challenges, though discouraging, are opportunities for growth and deeper understanding.

Many of us just need deliverance because we have deep-rooted things that we don't want to uncover or even know needs uncovering, but all we need to do is surrender it all to God. Too often, I've tried to control situations based on my own understanding, only to find myself frustrated and exhausted. I hate when I allow my feelings and emotions to get the best of me. I am still learning but sometimes I want my way and forget about Proverbs 3:5-6. I ask God for help always, but at times pride gets the best of me. I hate it when I allow the devil access, which allows him to toy with me and my husband. I have prayed and fasted a lot for my marriage and for my husband. We still face a lot of opposition today. But one thing I've realized in all of this is that we do not wrestle against flesh and blood but against rulers of the dark world. Spiritually, I would say I'm a little stronger, and it takes a lot to get me down because even when things get weary, I still put my trust in God. Sometimes seeing my husband struggle bothers me and becomes a distraction. But when I realize that it's the enemy's plan to put me down, that's when I start to really war in the spirit. Things are not always in our control, and we can't continue to stress about it. What we can control is what we do and how we react. I choose to read the Word. The bible says in Mathew 11:28 *"Then Jesus said, Come to me, all of you who are weary and carry heavy burdens, and I will give you rest."* This doesn't necessarily mean that the issue or problem will go away but when you give it to GOD, you have a supernatural peace about it. Then nothing will dissuade you as it did in the past because you have now given the control to GOD.

Before getting married, many people told me that marriage was hard, but I told myself that I knew that I could handle it. Becoming a wife was probably the worst and best thing that happened to me. (*I wasn't saying that in the beginning though*). I had to relearn a lot of things. I learned a lot about myself. My thinking had to change and even how I conversed with my husband had to change. I would say I was very demanding in the early stages of our marriage. Folks, this was a significant challenge for me. In the beginning, I just couldn't understand certain things and kept failing at a lot of others. I was stretched to the max. The warfare was serious. I am still faced with spiritual and psychological opposition, but I have learned to handle it better. I felt like I was an enemy of God. I kept asking Him why He allowed me to go through so much pain and confusion. I asked the Lord if I was missing something again. I assumed that I had my life together because I was rightfully and matrimonially complete, no longer living in sin. I was completely wrong. I've never prayed and fasted so much in my entire life. I went through pain that I never imagined I would face. I wanted my marriage to work, and even though divorce was not an option, I still felt like I wanted one at times. We both had many insecurities in so many areas. To be honest, I didn't want to deal with them. There was so much we

needed to learn, so much we needed to talk about and resolve. Ladies, there is power in your tongue; don't ever forget that. You can make or break someone with your words. There are times when we are upset, and we can literally uplift or cut another person down.

My husband and I come from 2 different upbringings so coming together as a couple brought many conflicts that I had never anticipated. There was so much that we needed to understand about each other, and to this day, I'm still learning. I'm not saying it gets easy, but it just gets better. You choose your battles. The ones that are too hard to manage alone, give them the Lord. I had to give several of our issues to the Lord because the burden was too heavy for me at times. Let me tell you, the power of prayer makes all things powerful and possible. There were times I didn't love my husband or couldn't stand him. I thought there was something wrong with me, but some well-experienced couples said it was normal. In that season there were many times I heard that marriage was not about what you can get but what you can give to your person. I prayed so much to God and asked Him to forgive me; forgive me for not knowing and not giving more to my husband. I asked the Lord to allow me to love my husband the way I should, as Christ loved me. I know in the Bible that the man is love his wife as Christ loves the church, but I felt that I had lacked so much in properly loving and supporting my husband, that I was desperate to cover the insufficiency in any way possible. I also requested that my husband love me the way he loved Christ (see Eph 5:21-33 for instructions on a Christian household between husband and wife). In time, I learned so much about myself and my capabilities.

My marriage is where I have consulted the Lord the most. I built an authentic personal relationship with God. In any relationship, we may allow our emotions to consume us, and we sometimes speak out of character. Remember, you can never take those words back. Be very mindful of what you say when you are upset. It is best to wait and cool off before communicating, especially if you know your words and even your actions may be very harsh. So, instead of arguing with my husband, I fought it out through prayer and waited to see the manifestation of those prayers take place. We can't continue to nag our spouses about the things that bother and annoy us, it will turn them off, especially when we have not properly communicated that those things bother and annoy us! At times, my emotions did get the best of me, but we always talked about how we could have handled the situation differently. I love my husband with ALL my heart, and though he has his flaws, I do too. I pray for him through it. I try to give him all my support. It isn't an easy task. I had to ask God for guidance in this. Sometimes it is hard to understand men, and only God can provide that wisdom and clarity. I had to let go of my pride; this had hindered us from reaching a different level in our relationship.

The Lord came to me one day when I was putting all the blame on my husband. He said, "It's not all about you. You must try and understand where he is coming from." That seriously humbled me. What followed was a tranquil season of reflection. The Lord asked me to just provide him the support that he needed. It is important to give men as many affirmations as possible, telling them that you appreciate them. My husband's love languages are words of affirmation and quality time. We must understand that men deal with many things internally, and it can be hard for them to show it, especially if they haven't learned how to properly express themselves. My husband has this idea in his head that he must be perfect in everything and for everyone, usually forgetting himself and his own needs. I constantly try to encourage him to go out, relax, and have some personal care but he believes that he always needs to be on the go. It's hard. There have been several occasions that I have had to forcefully make him go somewhere so that he can relax. I usually text my husband throughout the day to know how his day is and what his day may be like when he gets home; that way, he also knows I'm thinking of him. Every day, I intentionally ask him how he is doing and if there is anything that I can do to help and support him. Most of the time, it's a "no," but at least he knows I'm here should he need me. The enemy wants to separate us and break marriages so he will use even the smallest thing, such as a missed "hello" message. We can't fall into his trap. Yes, sometimes we can get so focused on our partners, and neglect ourselves in worrying about them and taking care of them. I sometimes forget about myself. In this season of my life, it seems as if all I am doing is being on the go. I am always pouring into people but forget myself in the process. I am learning to put myself first. Sometimes I get so consumed with my husband, children and everyone else, interceding on their behalf, and forget to petition for myself and the things that I desire God to do in my life. Just don't forget to consider yourself, reboot, command your day, and give it to God. He knows us best and He knows the whole outcome. Although, I find this hard at times, I just remind myself to pause and talk to the Holy Spirit about what it is that He wants me to do next. This way I'm not depending on myself, and I won't feel burned out and overwhelmed.

REFLECTIVE QUESTIONS

What are some significant challenges you've encountered in your marriage journey or relationship? How did these challenges shape your perspective on marriage?

_____

_____

_____

_____

Reflect on a time when you felt overwhelmed by marital responsibilities. How did prayer and seeking God's guidance help you navigate through that situation?

_____

_____

_____

_____

In what ways have cultural or societal expectations influenced your role as a wife? How do you reconcile these expectations with your personal beliefs and values?

_____

_____

_____

_____

Matthew 11:28 says, *"Come to me, all you who are weary and burdened, and I will give you rest."* How has surrendering your marriage challenges to God brought you peace and strength?

_____

_____

_____

_____

How do you balance supporting your spouse and taking care of your own needs? What strategies have helped you maintain this balance?

_____

_____

_____

_____

BIBLE VERSES

Matthew 19:6 *"So they are no longer two, but one flesh. Therefore, what God has joined together let no one separate."*

Hebrews 13:4 *"Give honor to marriage; one remains faithful one another in marriage. God will surely judge people who are immoral and those who commit adultery."*

CLOSING PRAYER:

Dear God, bless our marriage with unwavering love, patience in adversity, and joy in shared moments. Grant us the wisdom to appreciate each other's uniqueness, the strength to overcome challenges, and grace to continually grow together. May our commitment be a beacon of inspiration, reflecting the beauty of a sacred union. In Jesus' name I pray, Amen.

CHAPTER 14

TRANSPARENCY

This marriage has been the catalyst for my journey towards deeper faith and understanding. My marriage is the whole reason why I wanted to write a book of hope for women. I only say women because I am speaking from my perspective. We women see and hear things differently than men. So, let's get into it. After a year of marriage, I got fired from my job, at 9 months pregnant. We struggled! I had to get help from the state; I went on SNAP (food stamps) and state medical insurance. I never thought that something like that would or could ever happen to me because I went to college and obtained a bachelor's degree. Due to being pregnant I could not get another job. My husband was the breadwinner for a couple of years because the cost of childcare was also too expensive. When my son was about 18 months old, I went back to working again as a Medical Assistant and a Certified Nursing Assistant (CNA).

Before I came into my husband's life, he had his own habits on how to deal with stress. It was either smoking or drinking. I was not fully aware nor was I exposed to this growing up. After about a year I started to notice something strange. He would come home not himself and at times would get into random arguments with me when I asked him a question. With the comments he made, I believed that I could not be a good wife, and that I was always doing something wrong. I felt awful. When I would go out to purchase things for my son, like diapers or food, my card would get denied. Then I started to check the bank account we had together and noticed several large purchases at the liquor store. We were nearly broke. Any confrontation about it led to arguments. There were times I had to ask my younger siblings for assistance, and it was so embarrassing. AS I've mentioned before, I was the oldest and felt that I should be supporting my siblings and not the other way around.

After doing some research, I realized that my husband was addicted to alcohol. That's how he coped with life's situations. I had never had anyone in my family or close to me deal with this. For 3 years, I had dreams of my husband in a casket. I would see a dark image at the foot of the bed. He was dark, dressed in black with red eyes. Because I was not very familiar with the spiritual realm, I didn't know what it was, but it made me feel uneasy. Years later after taking an intercessory prayer class, I found out it was the spirit of death waiting at my husband's footstool. After watching the movie "War Room," I took authority over my house and prayed against the plans of the enemy for my home, my marriage and my husband. My husband continued to struggle for years. I wanted to leave him because it was too much, and it was almost unbearable. There were times that he threatened to harm himself though I believe it was a form of Manipulation and a cry for attention. My husband also coped by cutting himself. Being under the influence of alcohol enhanced his emotions and he couldn't handle it at times because he was not taught how. I tried to show him love in every possible way. I would send him Bible Verses and speak words of affirmation for him to know that he was cared for and loved. In his early 20's he used alcohol to ease his mind until it became a problem. I didn't understand what he was going through because I never experienced being around anyone in his condition. I often tried to talk to him whether he was under the influence or not, about what we could do to help but it didn't work. He was under the spirit of Pharmekia. Google's meaning of pharmekia states that it is the use of drugs and means a drug, charm, enchantment."

He often blamed me for his drinking. The more and more I thought about it, the more I believed him and felt it was my fault. So, expressing myself or any concerns made me scared of what it would do to him. I started walking on eggshells and did not want to be the cause of him picking up a drink. It was hard. I felt so alone. I didn't share this with anyone. The only ones who knew were my immediate family. Because I loved this man, and I didn't want him to be mistreated by my family or friends. I questioned God and asked Him again why was He punishing me. I asked Him what did I do to deserve this treatment and such a miserable life. For 2 years I isolated myself from everyone and activities from church. I was depressed. I no longer wanted to be in the marriage. I felt like I was set up, because who I had learned hm to be (OR Use this who I came to know was not who he had showed me in the beginning although there may have been signs I ignored) was not who he had showed me in the beginning.

REFLECTIVE QUESTIONS

Have you ever faced unexpected challenges in your marriage or relationships that tested your faith? How did you cope?

_____

_____

_____

What role did prayer play in navigating your toughest moments?

_____

_____

_____

How did you learn to balance personal challenges while supporting your spouse?

_____

_____

_____

In what ways have your experiences shaped your understanding of marriage as a covenant before God?

_____

_____

What lessons have you learned about communication and conflict resolution in your relationship?

BIBLE VERSES

Philippians 4:6-7 *"Do not be anxious about anything, but in every situation, by prayer and petition, with thanksgiving, present your requests to God. And the peace of God, which transcends all understanding, will guard your hearts and your minds in Christ Jesus."*

Matthew 19:6 *"So they are no longer two, but one flesh. Therefore, what God has joined together, let no one separate."*

John 10:10 *"The thief comes only to steal and kill and destroy; I have come that they may have life and have it to the full."*

CLOSING PRAYER

Heavenly Father, I acknowledge Your greatness and trust in Your power to bring victory and breakthrough in my life. Lord, You are the God of the impossible, the One who makes a way where there seems to be no way. I ask for Your divine intervention in every area of my life, especially in my marriage and all my relationships. Father, I pray for victory over every challenge, every obstacle, and every battle that stands in the way of Your perfect will for my life. I claim Your promise that no weapon formed against me will prosper (Isaiah 54:17), and I stand firm in the assurance that I am more than a conqueror through Christ who strengthens me (Romans 8:37). In my marriage and relationships, I pray for Your blessing, peace, and unity. Lord, strengthen the bond between me and my spouse, my family, my friends, and all those whom You have placed in my life. May our relationships be built on love, trust, and mutual respect. Teach us to honor one another, to communicate with kindness, and to forgive freely as You have forgiven us. I pray for breakthrough in areas where I feel stuck, discouraged, or defeated. Let Your light shine in every dark place and bring healing to any and all brokenness. I trust that You will open doors that no one can shut and close those that are not part of Your plan for my life. Lord, I ask that You empower me to be an overcomer in all things, with Your strength. In my relationships, I pray for Your wisdom to guide my words and actions. I place my life, my marriage, and all my relationships into Your hands, knowing that You are the ultimate source of victory and breakthrough and peace. I trust You, Lord, and I thank You for the victory that is already mine in Christ Jesus. In Jesus' name I pray, Amen.

CHAPTER 15

BEING SET FREE! SURRENDERING MY WILL TO GOD

On my way home to work one day, I heard the Lord. He said, why have you made your husband your idol? Have I ever forsaken you? I told him no, and from that day, I started to live again. Even in my darkest moments, God visited me even when I didn't ask. I started praying and fasting for my husband. This went on for about 5 to 6 years. After joining a group at church, I was able to share my pain with a few friends from church. At the time, I was on the verge of losing my mind. I felt like I was out of touch with everything. But when I finally shared my pain, the loss, the loneliness, the hurt, I felt liberated. The weight I was carrying was lifted, and the headache left my mind. I no longer felt like I needed to be institutionalized. My feelings were validated. I realized that Geno's drinking was not my fault, but he used me to justify his actions. He chose to use that to cope, and it had nothing to do with me. As his wife, I felt it was up to me to get him help. I tried getting him professional help, but it didn't work. I asked his family for help, but they didn't really understand the severity of the situation until I showed them pictures of the bruises he had from drinking. I tried seeing if my church would help but it was not what I expected. They were judgy and pulled us out of programs and groups. I didn't like how they isolated us. He couldn't connect with them, and they didn't understand. It hurt a lot because all I wanted to do is save my husband. I was desperate to find help and support for him, but I didn't want people judging him. My husband is a good man but was a slave to this thing and I just wanted him to be free. I had nothing and no one else I could go to after trying to handle this issue on my own, so I went back to God and His timing. Surrendering my control to God was the hardest yet most liberating decision I made. It meant trusting God's timing and His Plan, even when the circumstances are bleak.

In 2014 My husband tried to stop. He was good for about 6 months, until he started up again. After attending a friend's wedding, he drank for 6 days, and he was stuck. As I looked in my husband's eyes he seemed like a prisoner and was lost. It's like he was calling for help but couldn't reach out and grasp it, so I had to step in. I called a couple of rehab places and was able to find one in Florida that was willing to take him the same day. I told his family what was happening, and his older brother came to speak to him, but he was nearly mentally gone. I packed his suitcase, a notebook and his bible. I left him a note to write in the notebook daily to talk about what his experience was like. I had to physically go to the gate with him at the airport to make sure he got on the plane. I was at my wits end; this was the last thing I could think of that would save him and our marriage. At the time we only had 2 kids. They were 5 and 2 years old. For 30 days I had to depend on God for his breakthrough. I worshiped and prayed for him daily. It was hard. I felt alone. I cried most nights. I thought that when he left, I would feel fine, but I wasn't. I felt guilty like I made a bad decision and I didn't know how he was going to truly feel about me afterward.

When he returned, we tried to pick up where we left off prior to the serious issues and work things out as a couple. We started to talk about how we were going to allow God to use us for His Kingdom. Before all of this I had a lot of dreams, and it was always me fighting and standing in the gap for my husband. Geno came back on fire for God and was different. For 4 years he held out. During that time, sometimes we were fighting together in my dreams. Then he was betrayed by someone he trusted and that messed him up. This was a man of God that he looked up to. He took advantage of Geno and the gifts he had. The betrayal shattered his sense of self, and he went back to drinking heavily. This drinking has been a long battle for us. I know for sure God is and will deliver him. I will continue to lean on the Lord and be a woman and a wife of prayer.

REFLECTIVE QUESTIONS

How have you learned to surrender control to God in your relationship?

_____
_____
_____
_____

What strategies have helped you navigate setbacks and disappointments?

_____
_____
_____
_____

Do you have a family or friend who struggles? How have you helped them, or do you feel you need to step back?

_____
_____
_____
_____

If you've experienced this, how has it shaped or molded you as a person?

_____
_____
_____
_____

BIBLICAL VERSES:

Romans 12:12 *"Be joyful in hope, patient in affliction, faithful in prayer."*

1 Thessalonians 5:17 - *"Pray continually."*

Ephesians 6:18 - *"And pray in the Spirit on all occasions with all kinds of prayers and requests. With this in mind, be alert and always keep on praying for all the Lord's people."*

CLOSING PRAYER

Dear God, thank You for Your faithfulness and grace in my life and marriage. In the midst of life's challenges, God You have been my rock and my refuge. You have turned my pain into a testimony of Your love and redemption. My marriage is a work in progress, but I am thankful for the growth and healing we've experienced together. Help me to trust You more fully, knowing that You are always with us, guiding and sustaining us through every season. Grant us wisdom, patience, and a heart of compassion as we navigate the challenges of life together. May our marriage be a reflection of Your love and grace, bringing glory to Your name. In Jesus' name I pray, Amen.

CHAPTER 16

HOPE RESTORED

I wrote this book because I almost lost all my hope, BUT GOD! God guided me through it all. I mean the enemy was at work. He wanted me dead, so he used my husband to get me, but he failed. He wanted my husband dead and used alcohol to try to get him and destroy our marriage, But he failed, and my husband is still here. We both have overcome so much. His drinking and my worry are what turned me into a prayer (Although I believe I've had this gift early on). Things aren't perfect but they are much better. I have learned to fight through prayer and fasting. I'm not perfect and I'm no longer trying to fix my husband because only God can. I am learning to listen, use wisdom, and understand that sometimes God has to fully remove you from what you know and are comfortable with for there to be a true change. My desire is that he lives and lives for God. I'm no longer yelling and starting an argument or asking him why he drinks because this is bigger than me and him. When I am worried and stressed, I call on God for His guidance and how I can support him. I realized that he already feels low and worthless. He knows that he has a problem and often feels helpless and powerless to overcoming it. It's best to keep my mouth shut. I'm not going to lie, there are times as a human being when the flesh wants to lash out. The Holy Spirit has warned me on several occasions not to engage. Sometimes I don't listen and pay for it when things escalate. The Lord had to tell me that it's not all about me and I needed to humble myself and be his support. The circumstances and trauma we face can cause us to use people or substances to try to overcome them, but they are not always healthy solutions because you never feel fully satisfied and want more. So, when my human nature and flesh no longer want to be with my husband, and I found it too hard to watch him struggle in this situation, I look to God. Even though it still hurts to see that it's so hard for him to be completely free, healed, and delivered, I look to God. Through the midst of this I asked God to show me how to love my husband and be there for him. I asked Him to allow me to see my husband through His eyes and vice versa.

During COVID we had to make another hard decision for him to leave for Rehab because the situation had once again become very bad. He was miserable and I felt so bad. We sat the kids down and told them that he had to leave again. By this time, we had 4 kids and the 3 oldest understood because they had been praying for him. We try our best to keep our children in the loop because we want to break generational curses. I had tried to protect them, but I couldn't. They have eyes and ears and are also children of God who ask a lot of questions. I didn't want to lie to them and hinder their own natural and spiritual growth.

When the decision was made to return to rehab, I had to reason with the hubby. Instead of blaming and picking a fight I had to look at my husband deeply. I started to think of his childhood and the many experiences he had. The biggest challenge for him was balancing the responsibilities of being both a husband and a father. He felt he had to use alcohol to cope with all the hurt and pain. Healing needed to take place. I started to calm down, observe, and reflect. My motto became, if I don't have anything nice to say don't say it at all because you can't take your words back. I couldn't sit here and attack him with the same mouth I used to say I love you with. For those who know me, when I'm passionate about something it comes off very strong and assertive and not everyone takes that well. So, I went with a gentler approach and started speaking to him as a friend and started to speak life into him. I waited when he was sober and then we would talk. Even with the pain of seeing Geno in this position, I never stopped loving him. I loved him more because at times I felt some of his pain and I just wanted to shower him with all the love I had inside. I wanted our marriage to last, not just for me, but for him, our children, and our faith. I let him know that not only did I deeply love him but so did our children. We communicated and expressed our feelings to him in whatever way we thought he would receive it. Communication is so important. It is the only way to have a successful marriage or relationship with anyone.

What is Communication? The imparting or exchanging of information or news. So you are transmitting, presenting, imparting or conveying thoughts, ideas, facts, opinions, etc. My husband and I have very difficult and tough conversations which help us understand each other more and get past hurt to receive healing. I used to make threats of leaving and sometimes that stressed him out more making him feel even more incomplete. I had to step aside and look at my mistakes and faults too, even though I was in denial. I really didn't want to acknowledge or deal with myself. When you're married, it's important to connect and share some issues with married folks you trust, because only they can understand what it is you're facing and give sound advice. God also sends people by your side to learn and observe so they can know how to pray for their future spouse. You want to have people who are going to pray you through, not people who are looking at your situation outwardly and simply telling you to leave instead of considering the deeper internal aspects and complexities involved. In all situations, you have to use wisdom.

Marriage is a commitment that requires. It's a covenant you made in front of God. A covenant is an agreement between God and His people, in which God makes promises to His people requiring certain conduct and conditions from them. The same grace and favor that God has upon you when you have done wrong in his eyes is the same grace you should be extending to your spouse. At times we play the blame game and refuse to examine ourselves. What are you lacking? What is it that God needs to deliver out of you? I had to learn the hard way as I was throwing stones at my husband. I wasn't paying attention to the way I spoke to him when he shared his concerns with me. Honestly, I didn't understand how he could feel those ways. I had to put in the work to start leaning on the Holy Spirit so things would start to look and feel clearer. Today my relationship is a lot different then what it used to look and feel before. We still have a lot of work to do and if there has been an argument or misunderstanding between us, we RESET. Webster's meaning of Reset means to set again and anew. Instead of holding a grudge, being upset, and having unforgiveness, we rest our focus to God so we don't hinder His help and blessing. God isn't focused on our fleeting feelings; He only cares about our obedience. In Philippians 4:6-7 it says, *"do not be anxious about anything, but in everything by prayer and supplication with thanksgiving let your requests be made known to God. And the peace of God, which surpasses all understanding, will guard your hearts and your minds in Christ Jesus."*

My question to you is do you love your husband or wife? If so, are you willing to fight for them? If that is a yes, stop arguing and get into prayer; it is your most powerful weapon. If you were going through a rough time and didn't know how to get out of it, would you want someone you love or cared about to extend their hand to you? Now take out a notebook and ask the Holy Spirit what is going on with them and what is going on with you? Ask Him to show you how to pray and what to pray for. After you finish, show your loved one support in whatever that they are doing or that's meaningful to them. Say with your mouth that you got their back. Remember we don't wrestle against flesh and blood but principalities and rulers of this dark world. The enemy is on assignment to separate you! He wants to confuse you. He does not want to see Heterosexual (man and woman) people successfully married together. He is only here to kill, steal and destroy. John 10:10 says, *"The thief comes only to steal and kill and destroy; I have come that they may have life, and have it to the full."* God wants you to be filled with his abundance! Don't allow your emotions to cloud your judgment. Feelings are temporary and don't last. What does God say? He is everlasting, nothing is impossible to turn around. You can still win and be victorious.

REFLECTIVE QUESTIONS

What are things lacking in your marriage or relationships? How can you improve yourself in order to improve your relationship?

_____

_____

_____

_____

What steps are you taking to cultivate a deeper connection with God and your spouse?

_____

_____

_____

_____

In what ways do you see God unfolding in your marriage?

_____

_____

_____

_____

Knowing how to communicate efficiently with others is very important. Everyone receives information differently. Think about where you might be lacking in your communication skills. How do you communicate and receive information best? How does your partner? Once you know your styles, work on a communication plan for discussions, arguments, dating, traveling, etc.

_____

_____

BIBLE VERSES

Psalm 51:12 *"Restore to me the joy of Your salvation and uphold me with a willing spirit."*

2 Corinthians 4:8-9 *"We are afflicted in every way, but not crushed; perplexed, but not driven to despair; persecuted, but not forsaken; struck down, but not destroyed."*

Isaiah 41:10 *"Fear not, for I am with you; be not dismayed, for I am your God; I will strengthen you, I will help you, I will uphold you with My righteous right hand."*

James 1:19 *"Know this, my beloved brothers: let every person be quick to hear, slow to speak, slow to anger."*

CLOSING PRAYER

Heavenly Father,

I come to You with a heart seeking restoration and renewal. You are the Restorer, Healer, Rebuilder, and Promise Keeper. I ask You to restore the years that have been stolen by hardship, pain, or regret. Renew my strength, hope, and joy in Your presence and help me to see the beauty You are creating in the midst of brokenness. In hard times, it is easy to lose sight of You, Your faithfulness, and Your goodness. Help me to always remember You are with me. Please give me the courage to keep pushing as You prepare me for something greater. Let Your peace guard my heart and mind as I trust in You, Lord. Give me the humility to listen more than I speak and the patience to understand before I react. Let my words be words of healing and building others up, not of hurting or breaking them down. Guide me in times of conflict so that I can respond in love. Lord, fill me with Your love and let it be my foundation for everything I do. Teach me to love others as You have loved me. In Jesus' name I pray, Amen.

CHAPTER 17

MOTHERHOOD AND RAISING A FAMILY

Raising my 5 children has been an incredible journey filled with challenges and blessings. I'm so grateful to have been blessed with all my beautiful children. Despite having 5-Csections, I know nothing is impossible for God because He protected me through it all. The Lord covered me even when the enemy was plotting. My children are about 3 years apart. I didn't plan them. They all came at their appointed times. I choose to give them all biblical names because I want them to stand out and walk with purpose. I am my children's first prophet. I speak life into my children and rebuke any negative things that people may say about or over them. I have made it a habit of not calling them out their names because it could be truly detrimental to their identity since there is power in our words. As a youth, there were words said to me by family, church members, and friends that still affect who I am today. I may say you're acting like such and such and you need to change but I try my best and make a conscious effort to speak life over them so they will feel empowered.

As a parent, you can't really hide who you are. Children are always listening and watching, and ready to spread your business to others. They basically know you inside out and they make the greatest impressions. We are their biggest role models and the need us to guide and instruct them. I'm not going to lie, parenthood is frustrating especially, as they are growing up into pre-teens and teenagers. They become a lot sassier and spicier with their tongue. They fight, bully, tease, instigate, and interrogate each other. My parenting skills are different from my parents. We try to give our kids the ability to express themselves along with setting boundaries and limits. Sometimes they get a little too comfortable and entitled and I want to default to how I was raised in a Haitian household, but I show them love, patience, grace and give them time to sort their emotions.

PARENTING

I had a honeymoon baby. I was nervous the first time I found out I was pregnant. I was afraid that I would not be a good mother. But you know what, God always provides you with the wisdom and tools to raise your children right if you are willing. After seeing my first son Hezron, which means dart of joy, wisdom, and intuitiveness, for the first time, I was in love. It was easy raising him. He is such a bright kid and very intuitive. He is a leader and fills that role very well. He does not always realize how gifted and special he is. At times, people don't always understand him and may get annoyed with some of the things he does, just like they did with me. Occasionally, he lets fear get in the way of being used by God. I often encourage him to see the greatness he has within himself, and not to allow what others say about him affect his journey and walk with God. I want my children to confide in me before they do to anyone because I can pray for them and will always have their best interest at heart.

Being a first-time mother, I felt like I completely lost myself. I felt like I was only being used as a feeding machine. I couldn't really go out much because my son only wanted breast milk. At the time, I was dealing with postpartum depression. I ended up gaining 50 pounds. It almost felt like my job was only to be a mother. I felt stuck, lost my identity and individuality, and wanted to be free. I wanted to take care of myself and love myself once again. I am grateful that I had so much support from my family, so I was never alone, but motherhood is tough. You have to somehow balance everything out; trying to equally and successfully be a wife, a mother, a sister, a friend. When I had my second child, I felt even more overwhelmed. I named my daughter, Hadassah, which means Esther, signifying victory, compassion, resilience, and joy. I could name many more because the story of Esther was so powerful and inspiring, and I felt my daughter would one day emulate those attributes. However, I still questioned my abilities as a mother. She had a strong personality then and still has it now. She possesses an iron will and a headstrong determination, making her unwavering in her convictions. At the same time, she is deeply caring and strives to treat everyone with fairness and respect. Her genuine passion for the wellbeing of others shines through in everything she does, reflecting her compassionate and altruistic nature. I often prayed and asked God how to properly raise her and give her the affection and nurturing she needs. He showed me she requires affirmations to help build her confidence. I learned that the way that I disciplined my son couldn't be the same with her. She is easy to talk with after she cries it out and makes space for herself. She doesn't want to be spoken to when she is mad. I had to learn the hard way but after having better communication of her needs I was able to understand.

My third, Zephaniah, means Lord has concealed, protected, and treasured by God. She cries a lot but she is the sweetest person you will meet. She is very helpful when needed and has an old soul. She and her sister do not like to be yelled at but rather spoken to. When she is upset or has done something wrong, all she needs is a hug. I believe that gives her a sense of security that she is cared for. Believe it or not, it works, and she calms down after I say, "I love you". Parents don't let pettiness or pride get a hold of you. There were times that I was so upset that I didn't want to hug it out and would have chosen to remain upset. But I felt the conviction of the Lord and would hug her. We will always be their role models. It's not right that they move on, and we hold on to our feelings. I hope to love the same way that Christ shows that unconditional love towards us. At 7 years old she told me she wanted to be baptized. She was so excited about it. I almost told her she was too young. But recalled that I was also 7 years old when I was filled with the Holy Spirit. When I was excited to go to church and was sometimes dismissed, I felt misunderstood. I remember when I was 14 and wanted to get baptized but my father felt that I was too young to do it. I didn't want my daughter to feel discouraged and dismissed so I explained what baptism was and what it meant. We watched videos together to make sure she saw and understood what she was getting herself into. I pray that the Lord continues to transform her into the child and woman she is meant to be.

My fourth, Adonijah, which means My Lord is Yahweh, is so spontaneous. That boy keeps me on my toes. He is very determined. He is so full of so much energy that we all can't keep up with him. He doesn't always listen. I consider him to be the most challenging of all my kids so far. I know that his voice will be a weapon because when he screams, I feel a shaking in my spirit. I've asked the Lord why he is the way he is because sometimes I feel burnt out. Deep down I know that this is for a greater purpose of whatever the Lord may have in store for his future. We are trying to raise him despite the obstacles he will face. It won't be easy but at least he'll be more prepared. Adonijah Jahaziel "AJ" is a very smart and observant kid. You only have to teach him and show him things once. He is really like a sponge. He is a sweet boy and adores his baby sister. He can't seem to keep his hands off her. I look forward to seeing their bond grow as they get older.

My last child, Azriel, means God is my help. Although she is still so young there is a certain presence about her. She's very observant and a people person. I see so much greatness in her. She loves to smile and always seems so confident and physically strong. I call her Ms. CEO because she sits like a boss. She has a strong personality she is a "go getta". She is child number 5 and I see everyone's personality in her. She is younger and right now needs more emotional and physical support. All my husband and I ask of the Lord is to bring balance and guidance in dealing with them all. My husband and I often ask the Lord for guidance on dealing with them all.

Due to all their different personalities, ways of learning, and receiving information, I have often felt overwhelmed on how to discipline each of them. At times I tell them that I need a break, and most of the time, they understand. My oldest usually takes charge and keeps his siblings busy. There are times I want to escape. Sometimes it feels like too much, and I need to lean on the Lord for encouragement and guidance. Being a parent is a full-time job, there are no breaks or times off. Even at the worst moments in my life, I had to be present for my children, smiling, laughing, and playing with them as if nothing was happening. My children depend on me to be who they needed me to be for them at any given moment. There have been times I have yelled or said something that they didn't appreciate. The guilt affected me in ways that taught me to change how I was communicating and interacting with my kids. I still say I'm sorry when I'm wrong. I want my children to know that we are not perfect and everyone, young and old, make mistakes. So, I give room for us to often talk about options on a different approach or solution.

My husband and I try our best to teach the kids about Christ and His sacrifices for us, along with the benefits of having a personal relationship with Him. We have family devotion every night to teach the children about God. My husband and I face challenges finding time to spend with each other. The kids bud in on the times that we want to sit together on the couch. At times they do get jealous. My husband and I are now taking the initiative to travel alone yearly and go out at least once a month alone for dinner and other activities. Sometimes you get so caught up being a parent and forget about each other. It's essential to continue to keep that spark alive. If you ignore that, it could dampen your relationship. Remember, it was just the *two* of you before children came into the picture, and it will be the two of you after the children are grown and living their own lives.

REFLECTIVE QUESTIONS

How do you nurture your children's spiritual growth and relationship with God?

_____
_____
_____
_____

What strategies do you use to instill values and morals in your children's live?

_____
_____
_____
_____

How has parenting strengthened your own faith and reliance on God's guidance?

_____
_____
_____
_____

BIBLE VERSES

Proverbs 29:15 *"The rod of correction imparts wisdom, but a child left undisciplined disgraces its mother."*

Proverbs 22:6 *"Train up a child in the way he should go; even when he is old, he will not depart from it."*

CLOSING PRAYER:

Heavenly Father, I come before You as a parent, asking for Your wisdom and guidance in raising my child. Help me to train them in the way they should go, so that even as they grow older, they will not depart from Your truth. Grant me the strength and patience to offer correction in love, knowing that discipline imparts wisdom and shapes their character. May I lead with grace, and may my actions reflect Your heart, so my child may grow in wisdom and honor. Protect and guide them always, Lord, and give me the courage to parent with integrity. In Jesus' mighty name I pray, Amen.

CHAPTER 18

GODLY TIPS FOR KINGDOM FAMILIES

Here are some tools and tips on raising Godly children for the Lord's kingdom

1. **PRAYER**: It's important to incorporate prayer into your daily routine. Pray for your children's spiritual growth, wisdom, and protection. Teach them the importance of prayer and encourage them to develop their own relationship with God.

2. **BIBLE STUDY**: Make regular Bible study a family activity. Share stories, teachings, and principles from the Bible. Help your children understand the relevance of biblical teachings to their daily lives. We watch kid friendly YouTube skits that share stories about the bible.

3. **CHURCH**: Attend church services regularly as a family, even when you don't want to go. It's important to fellowship with others. Encourage your children to participate in age-appropriate activities and programs. Building a sense of community within a church can provide additional support and guidance.

4. **MODEL YOUR VALUES**: Children learn by example. Demonstrate the values and behaviors you want to instill in them. Show kindness, humility, forgiveness, and integrity in your life.

5. **FAMILY DEVOTIONS**: Set aside time for family devotions where you can read and discuss scripture together. This can be a

time for reflection, questions, and sharing insights. We do this as a family every night at 6pm.

6. **BUILD THEIR CHARACTER**: Emphasize the development of character traits such as honesty, responsibility, gratitude, and compassion. Use real life situations as teaching moments to instill these values.

7. **SERVICE AND OUTREACH**: Engage in community service and outreach activities as a family. Teach your children the importance of serving others and making a positive impact in the community. Lead by example. We have a lot of homeless people in our community and my children have seen me give to the homeless. They, in turn, have also given to the homeless with their own money freely.

8. **OPEN COMMUNICATION**: Create an environment where your children feel comfortable discussing their faith, doubts, and questions. Be open to answering their inquiries and guiding them through spiritual matters. Although they may seem like they are uncomfortable with you at first, keep pressing to show them that they can easily trust you. Try not to overreact so you don't scare them away. Share parts of your life, experiences, and struggles that relate to what they're going through so they don't feel alone and can also begin to see you as a valued and knowledgeable confidant. I always ask God for guidance.

9. **SET BOUNDARIES**: Establish clear expectations and boundaries based on biblical principles. Explain the reasons behind rules and guidelines and emphasize the importance of obedience and respect. My go to verses is Exodus 20:12

10. **ENCOURAGE INDIVIDUAL RELATIONSHIP WITH GOD**: Help your children build a personal relationship with God. Encourage them to pray, read the Bible, and seek God's guidance on their own. This can be done as a family by setting quiet time for like 30 minutes to get them to consecrate themselves in the presence of God.

11. **QUALITY TIME**: Spend quality time with your children. Building strong family bonds creates a foundation of trust and support, making it easier for children to embrace their faith. We like taking

them out one on one so they can have our undivided attention with each of us alone. You can also do an all-inclusive activity at home together by introducing a new hobby, playing games, watching a movie together, having an indoor picnic, or going for a walk. There is a variety of things you can do together.

Parents, always remember that every child is unique, and there's no single 'right' way to parent. These tips are a guide—adapt them to fit your child's individual needs and personality. If you need support, turn to God or seek advice from someone experienced in parenting.

PARENTAL PRAYER OVER YOURSELF

Father, In the name of Jesus, give me wisdom and guidance to parent the children you have provided to me. Guide me into embedding the Word of God in them. Help me to discipline them appropriately according to Your Word. Proverbs 22:6 says "Train up a child in the way he should go; even when he is old, he will not depart from it." Help me not to discipline them in anger and frustration. Allow me to be fair and not show favor over one child than the other. Give me a sound mind and allow me to teach that soundness to my children through my actions. Father, give me the discernment to know what's wrong with them and to be there for them when they need me the most. I don't want to be petty. Allow me to love them unconditionally, the same way You love me. Give me the ability to be strong and confidence to discipline them correctly so they can be good stewards in this world. Show me Your ways Lord when I get stuck. Give me the words to uplift them and not destroy them so they can trust me and tell me all about their fears and worries. When they share with me, whether it's good or bad, be my mouthpiece as I respond to them. Allow my actions to be pure and sincere. In Jesus Name I pray Amen!

REFLECTIVE QUESTIONS

If you have children, how do their personalities affect the way you parent?

_____
_____
_____
_____
_____
_____
_____

How can you improve as a parent? What things do you think you can do differently?

_____
_____
_____
_____
_____
_____
_____
_____

How do you currently communicate with your children? Do you think there is room for improvement? How so?

CHAPTER 19

PAIN TO POWER

Y ou Got The Power!

P - Prepare through prayer and devotion.

O - Overcome obstacles with faith.

W - Walk in God's will and purpose.

E - Equip yourself with the Word.

R - Renew your mind and spirit daily

BIBLE VERSE

"But you will receive power when the Holy Spirit comes on you; and you will be my witnesses in Jerusalem, and in all Judea and Samaria, and to the ends of the earth."
— **Acts 1:8**

DAILY AFFIRMATIONS

Daily Affirmations are what I use to start my day. You don't have to say all of them every day, but you can start with saying at least one every day. Maybe say it throughout the day to continue to encourage yourself. You'll soon find that as you read the scriptures, you may find new and different words of affirmation to empower yourself. One more thing I would like to add is speak with conviction and authority. Remember, this is your life and your loved ones. You want your adversary to know you mean business and you're not playing (you're not backing down)!

GENESIS 1:26

Then God said, "Let Us <u>make man in Our image</u>, according to Our likeness; and <u>let them rule</u> over the fish of the sea and over the birds of the sky and over the cattle and over all the earth, and over every creeping thing that creeps on the earth."

This verse is fire! From the beginning, God created you with this ability to rule with authority. So don't let the enemy put thoughts in your head that you can't do this or that or you're to shy to overcome. God gave you the power and it starts with you speaking it out loud! My desire is that you read these verses over and over and ask the Holy Spirit to help you understand them if they don't make sense to you yet.

24 BIBLICAL AFFIRMATIONS TO GET THROUGH THE DAY.

1. Today I will slay any opposition that comes against me (*Romans 12:19*)
2. I cancel the spirit of laziness and procrastination out of my life in Jesus' name! (*John 9:4, Philippians 4:13*)

3. I am chosen and anointed *(Deuteronomy 14:2)*
4. I am not a failure I am an overcomer *(1 Peter 5:7, 1 John 5:4)*
5. I am more than a conqueror *(Romans 8:37)*
6. I'm too blessed to be stressed *(1 Peter 5:8)*
7. I have the abundant life *(John 10:10)*
8. I am and will not be shaken in the name of Jesus *(Matthew 4:4)*
9. I have the righteousness of God *(Philippians 3:9, Romans 8:28, 10:17, 12:2)*
10. I will walk in power and destiny *(2 Timothy 1:7, Jeremiah 29:11, Habakkuk 2:3)*
11. I am beautiful, fearfully and wonderfully made *(Psalms 139:14)*
12. I will accomplish what I set out to do for myself and my family *(Romans 12:1-2, Philippians 3:12-14)*
13. I will walk with purpose *(John 3:16-17)*
14. I am not a slave to fear *(Isaiah 41:10, Psalms 118:6)*
15. I can do all things through Christ who gives me strength *(Philippians 4:13, Isaiah 43:2)*
16. God has given me the power to dominate my environment *(Luke 10:19)*
17. I will walk in victory this season *(Psalms 1:1, James 1:12)*
18. I have the peace of God *(Romans 5:1, John 14:27)*
19. This is my year of breakthrough and new beginnings *(Matthew 5:3-7, Hebrews 4:12, Isaiah 43:19)*
20. No weapon formed against me shall prosper *(Isaiah 54:17, Deuteronomy 20:1)*
21. My family is blessed *(Ephesians 1:3, Luke 11:28)*
22. Joy is mine! I am covered by the blood of Jesus *(1 John 5:14-15)*
23. I am not afraid, and I have self-discipline *(Isiah 41:8-10)*
24. The Lord will fight my battles *(Exodus 14:14)*

If you're feeling negatively about yourself or about a situation, speak the opposite. Don't let the enemy win. No matter who you are or where you've been there's greatness inside of you.

Anything that comes to mind, declare and decree it over your life. Even if you don't get the outcome you want, continue to declare positive words over you and those you hold close.

For example, *I will pass the exam today in Jesus's name!*

What affirmations do you speak over yourself:

- _____
- _____
- _____
- _____
- _____

REFLECTIVE QUESTIONS

In what way can you effectively integrate these affirmations into your daily routine?

_____
_____
_____
_____

What role does faith play in overcoming challenges and setbacks?

_____
_____
_____
_____

BIBLE VERSE

Genesis 1:26 *"Then God said, 'Let Us make man in Our image, according to Our likeness; let them have dominion over the fish of the sea, over the birds of the air, and over the cattle, over all the earth and over every creeping thing that creeps on the earth."*

CLOSING PRAYER:

Heavenly Father, thank You for Your promises and for equipping me with strength and courage through Your Word. Help me to consistently declare Your truths over my life and to trust in Your plans for me. May these affirmations be a source of encouragement and faith for others as well. In Jesus' name I pray, Amen.

CHAPTER 20

PRAYER & FASTING

There are so many ways to go about praying and fasting. Matthew 7:7-8

What is *Prayer*? Prayer is an *invocation* or act that seeks to activate a *rapport* with an object of worship through deliberate *communication*. The term refers to an act of supplication and intercession directed towards a deity. In layman's terms, prayer is a conversation with God.

Invocation is the action of appealing to or calling earnestly for something or someone for assistance or as an authority.

Rapport is close and harmonious relationship in which the people or groups concerned understand each other's feelings or ideas and communicate well.

Communication is the imparting or exchanging of information or news.

God is your friend. Prayer is communication with God where you have dialogue with Him. You acknowledge who He is, you talk and ask questions, but you need to give Him a chance to answer. That's why it's important to set aside quiet time with Him so you can hear Him. He speaks in a small calm voice. Prayer can be done in your own way. Everyone's relationship with God is different. You will develop your own style. Your prayer closet can be in your car, your bathroom, a closet, or anywhere you have "me or alone" time. Whatever allows you to connect with God, do it.

I tried so many fasts and fasted a lot through these tough times. Fasting allowed me to get closer to Christ. Starving the flesh and not putting worldly things into my mind or body allowed me to hear God better. That quiet time is everything. Fasting is also good for the body because it helps detox it from the chemicals and food, we put in it. Every time we feel hungry during the fast, we should be feeding it with the word of God. When you read the word it's important to pray. Ask the Holy Spirit to *reveal* and *illuminate* the scriptures for you so that it could be more understandable.

What is Fasting? It is a spiritual observance abstaining from all or some kinds of food, drink, media, or anything that occupies your mind and body more than God

Fasting is a necessity! It's not optional! There's something that needs to be produced in you. When you submit to the Lord He will work through you.

Types of Fasting: Each one of these fasts should be done with an attitude of humility and hunger for God. (Christian Disciplines by Julia Oates). When you are fasting, you should be engaging in the word of God to edify your mind. You should be feeding yourself God's word so you can be equipped for whatever life or the enemy throws at you. This means you should avoid watching TV, playing video games, using social media, or talking on the phone with friends, as these can become distractions. They may lead you to hear or discuss things that detract from your time of consecration. Fasting calls for dying to self and setting aside earthly urges to fully dedicate your time to God. Time is a precious gift—once it's gone, it cannot be reclaimed. Also, be very mindful of your health. If you need to make modifications to a fast due to your health, please be wise in taking care of your body while you follow God's Word.

Complete Fasting: You only drink water. (Isaiah 58:6)

Partial Fasting: Is when you refrain from eating from sunup to sundown. For example, 6:00am to 6:00pm. You can move the time to whatever works for you. Also, be mindful of your health. (Acts 13:2, 14:23)

Absolute Fasting: You do not eat or drink anything during this fast. You should not exceed 3 days of this fast. (Acts 9:9)

The Daniel Fast: This fast is taken from Daniel 10:2-3. In this fast, you only eat fruits, nuts, vegetables, and water to flush out toxins. No dairy and no animal products.

Sexual Fasting: Comes from Paul. He poses the idea that through mutual consent you would be apart for a time to devote yourself to praying. (1 Corinthians 7:3-6)

Corporate Fasting: Corporate fasting can be done in a variety of different ways with people. It can be done with your church, a Bible study group, your spouse, and so on. Your group can decide what kind of fast you will be doing and for how long. (Acts 13:2-3)

Soul Fasting: Is where you abstain from a certain area of your life that may be out of balance or something you consume much of your time. (Isaiah 25:1). Ideas for soul fasting include but are not limited to television, social media, podcasts, magazines, video games, and sports.

WHAT IS THE PURPOSE OF FASTING?

The intent behind fasting is to refrain from something for a certain amount of time with the purpose of growing our dependence on God and showing Him our need and desire for Him. Fasting is an act of discipline and sacrifice. (Wikipedia)

Fasting is a commitment between you and God. No one needs to know that you are fasting. No need to put on an act or tell lies. (Matthew 6:18)

HAVE YOU EVER FASTED BEFORE? YES OR NO

If Not, What Stopped You? Can you see Yourself committing to any of the above Fasts?

_____

_____

_____

_____

REFLECTIVE QUESTIONS

What role does quiet time play in hearing from God?

___

___

___

___

How can you cultivate a more consistent and meaningful prayer life?

___

___

___

___

In what ways has God answered your prayers or spoken to you during times of fasting?

___

___

___

___

BIBLICAL VERSES

Matthew 7:7-8 - *"Ask, and it will be given to you; seek, and you will find; knock, and it will be opened to you. For everyone who asks receives, and the one who seeks finds, and to the one who knocks it will be opened."*

Isaiah 58:6 *"Is not this the fast that I choose: to loose the bonds of wickedness, to undo the straps of the yoke, to let the oppressed go free, and to break every yoke?"*

CLOSING PRAYER

Heavenly Father,

I come before You in humility, setting aside time to fast and seek Your presence more deeply. I recognize that I am nothing without You, and I long to hear Your voice clearly. As I fast, I pray that You would quiet my heart and mind and remove any distractions so I can focus solely on You. Lord, I offer this time of sacrifice to You. Let it be an offering of worship and devotion. Strengthen me to endure through this fast as I draw closer to You. Let every hunger pang remind me of my dependence on You and let my longing for food be transformed into a deeper hunger for Your Word and Your presence. Let my flesh submit to Your Spirit, for I know my flesh desires to go against Your Spirit, and the Spirit is against the flesh (Galatians 5:16-17). I desire to do good but sometimes my flesh struggles because of the power of sin. Lord, help me not to get discouraged as I fast and seek You. Open my ears to hear from You. Speak to me clearly, whether through Your Word, Your Spirit, or through those You place in my path. I trust that You hear me, Father, and I trust that You will speak. Give me the wisdom to discern Your voice and the courage to follow wherever You lead. I believe that as I draw near to You, You will draw near to me. In Jesus' name I pray, Amen.

CHAPTER 21

DAILY DEVOTIONS

There are so many apps and books out there that can help you stay on track. I usually use Christian-based books so that my desires are aligned. Usually, I do devotions on what I may be feeling during the season. You can look into books that have timely, as in daily or weekly, devotions. This will allow you to stay disciplined, consistent, and on track. You can listen to podcasts, sermons, and inspirational motivators to start your day. I enjoy meditating with God. It's sitting in a quiet place with a pen and paper, closing your eyes and allowing the Lord to speak and then writing those ideas down.

READING BOOKS TO MOTIVATE & ELEVATE

The Battlefield of the Mind by Joyce Meyers

Overcoming Rejection by Frank Hammond

Lies That Women Believe: And the Truth That Sets Them Free By Nancy Leigh DeMoss

Kingdom Woman By Tony Evans

Lord Teach Us To Pray- By Gideon Andrew Thompson

The 40 Day Soul Fast: Your Journey to Authentic Living By Cindy Trimm

Rules of Engagement By Cindy Trimm

Prayers that Rout Demons: Prayers for Defeating Demons And Overthrowing the Powers of Darkness By John Eckhardt

The Gifts of the Holy Spirit By Dr. Rodney Howard-Browne

These are some of the books I have used to help guide me. There are many other books to choose from. Some of these books also come with their own recommendations as well. You can ask for other resources from people in your own circle.

CONNECTING WITH LIKE-MINDED PEOPLE

If the people you hang around are toxic, leave them because they could be hindering your growth and blessings. Connect with people who have your best interest at heart. There may be a friend, co-worker, or church member that you connect with.

Speak to them on the phone weekly.

Form a small prayer group or a group to just connect!

Get an accountability partner, someone you can trust and depend on. This partner has to be willing to be honest if you are slipping up and vice versa.

Connect with those who are already walking in what you want to accomplish. Learn from them.

Look up conferences that encourage women and talk about empowerment. It can also be about what you want to accomplish. You just have to be proactive in getting yourself into anything that will allow you to reach whatever goals you have written down or put your mind to.

CHAPTER 22

WALKING IN VICTORY!

ACHIEVING YOUR DREAMS WITH GOD'S PROVISION

PSALMS 40:1-5

> *"I waited patiently for the Lord to help me, and He turned to me and heard my cry. 2 He lifted me out of the pit of despair, out of the mud and the mire. He set my feet on solid ground and steadied me as I walked along. 3 He has given me a new song to sing, a hymn of praise to our God. Many will see what He has done and be amazed. They will put their trust in the Lord. 4 Oh, the joys of those who trust the Lord, who have no confidence in the proud or in those who worship idols. 5 O Lord my God, You have performed many wonders for us. Your plans for us are too numerous to list."*

Congratulations! I'm so glad you made it this far. I know it may have been hard to reflect on your life and your past. You had to revisit some things that you thought were behind you but found out that you needed more healing. That's because you are now becoming a better version of yourself. Through Christ all things are possible. I shared some personal things about myself and marriage which was not easy. I want you to know that you are not alone and there is no situation or circumstance that God cannot fix. Sometimes we want to see the change directly with our eyes but know that God hears you and He is working things on your behalf. He has not forgotten you! Call on the name of Jesus and stop fighting this battle alone. The only way I was able to get through any of this with a sound mind was only through Jesus. I had to stop being in control and allow him to control the situation and when I did that, I was liberated, and it felt good. Every time we take on burdens by ourselves, we are putting Jesus' back on the cross. He didn't die for us to carry it all.

What things have you learned about yourself and what *will you try to do* differently?

_____

_____

_____

_____

HOW TO SUCCEED AND BECOME A BETTER VERSION OF YOURSELF

A) Believe that You are an Overcomer & a Conqueror- Though you have been through opposition and pain, you haven't allowed it to stop you. You haven't accepted defeat. I know it was hard, you felt alone and may have had some sleepless nights, but you made it. You are ready to slay. You are ready to prove everyone wrong. You are to prove God right! You are somebody, you are a Child of God.

Say this prayer with me:

Father, in the name of Jesus, help my unbelief, allow me to walk in power, and believe that I am Victorious and walking in Victory. I believe that I am a Conqueror. For I am an overcomer, regardless of how people view me or what my past may be. I will see You through in every situation I face. Lord, You are my Redeemer and Restorer of ALL things. In Jesus Name I Pray, Amen.

B) Hold Yourself Accountable- You are responsible for your actions. You are responsible of your own reactions and decisions that help determine who you are and what your life can be. You are responsible to improve your relationships and turn your situations around. Admit when you're wrong. Admit if you made a mistake. Don't let pride overtake you. You can make the first move. Let your mind and your spirit be free from guilt and shame. Let it go. Don't hinder yourself.

Say this prayer with me:

Father, in the name of Jesus, I'm determined to be free. I will make better choices according to the Word of God. I acknowledge that I am not perfect and may have fallen short in living up to my values. Grant me the wisdom to recognize my mistakes and the humility to learn from them. May I be honest with myself about my strengths and weaknesses, and may I take responsibility for the impact I have on those around me. I won't allow unforgiveness and bitterness to consume me. I will walk in peace and freedom. I will hold my head up high and walk in righteousness. I am as bold as a lion. I have an abundant life. I have victory over my circumstances. I have the power to make a difference. In Jesus Name I Pray, Amen.

C) Have Unstoppable Faith- *"What good is it? Dear brothers and sisters, if you have faith but don't show it by your actions? Can that kind of faith save anyone?"* James 2:14 (NLT)

You may have heard people say to do it blindly, do it afraid, well this is what that means. You have to have faith and while you wait for things to happen you must believe and you must pray until something happens. There's no time for doubt and talking negatively about it not happening the way that you want it to. God has His own timing for everything.

For example, you can't pray and ask God for a job without looking for one. You have to put in the work. Filling out job applications, advertising yourself and scheduling interviews.

Say this prayer with me:

Father, in the name of Jesus, I can do all things through You who gives me strength. Your Word says if I believe, everything is possible. For we live by Faith not by sight. I am unstoppable. I am unshaken. I am driven. I put my trust in You. I cancel the spirit of doubt, double mindedness and confusion out of my mind. I am a new creation. Your word says "Teach me Your way, Lord, that I may rely on Your faithfulness; give me an undivided heart, that I may fear Your name. In Jesus Name I Pray, Amen.

D) Trust in The Power of Prayer- *"Do not be anxious about anything, but in every situation, by prayer and petition, with thanksgiving, present your requests to God."* Philippians 4:6 (NLT)

Pray until something happens (P.U.S.H.) There is true POWER in prayer. Sometimes a prayer request is fulfilled right away and sometimes it is delayed. Prayer is your communication with God. It's where you share your deepest and most intimate thoughts with God. It is when you can fully be yourself because God knows you best. Cast your worries and frustrations on Him because He cares for you. Be honest and transparent. He knows your heart deeply, but He wants you to admit to things. He didn't die on the cross for us to carry these burdens. The battle isn't ours, it's the Lord's.

Say this prayer with me:

Dear Heavenly Father, I come before You, acknowledging the truth of Genesis 1:26-28. I declare and decree that, as Your creation, I am made in Your image and likeness. Grant me the wisdom and strength to exercise the authority and dominion You have bestowed upon me over my environment. May Your guidance lead me to fulfill the purpose You have set for me. Bless me with the ability to be fruitful and multiply in every aspect of my life. Let Your grace and favor be upon me, enabling me to subdue challenges and bring positive change. In Psalm 27:1 it says "The Lord is my light and my salvation—whom shall, I fear? The Lord is the stronghold of my life—of whom shall I be afraid?" I place my hope in You, knowing that my identity and authority are rooted in Your divine design. In Jesus' name I pray, Amen

E) Keep Pushing Even When You Don't Want To- There are times when what you want is at the tip of your fingers, but something keeps grabbing hold of your blessing. With so much failure and opposition you may not want to go on, but you must. So many people that you know and don't know, of are counting on you and rooting for you. You may be the key to your generation or bloodline. Maybe the Lord has called you to be a Generational Curse Breaker. The Victory from your struggles can pave the way for your bloodline and descendants. Think about your children and their children! You have a purpose to fulfill, and the enemy isn't happy. That's why there's so much opposition. Always know that there's a fighter in you. I always say to myself, the spirit is willing, but the flesh is weak, YOU CAN DO IT!

Say this prayer with me:

Dear God, in times of trial and challenge, grant me the strength to persevere. Help me find courage in the face of adversity, and may Your unwavering love be my anchor. Strengthen my resolve to endure and guide me on the path of perseverance. I pray for tenacity, Lord, as I face difficulties and obstacles. I pray for the endurance to withstand the storms of life. Let Your Grace be my sustenance, and may I emerge from challenges with newfound strength and resilience. In Your name, I seek the power to press on. Gracious God, teach me patience in moments of uncertainty and waiting. Give me the wisdom to trust Your timing and the resolve to endure setbacks. May I find solace in Your plan and strength to keep moving forward.

Lord, in my journey of faith, help me persevere when doubts creep in. Strengthen my belief in Your promises, and let Your word be a lamp to my feet. May I remain steadfast in my commitment to follow Your path, not after the challenges that may come my way. Heavenly Father, grant me tenacity in pursuing my goals and dreams. When obstacles seem insurmountable, impart in me the determination to press on. Help me learn and grow through each trial, knowing that with You, all things are possible. Guide me with Your light as I navigate through difficult times and grant me the wisdom to learn from them. I pray that I am stronger, wiser, and more resilient, knowing that You are with me every step of the way, In Jesus Mighty Name I Pray, Amen!

F) Believe You Can Achieve Whatever You Set Your Mind To- If you thought it, you can work towards it. Just be conscious of who you share your dreams, visions, and goals with. Not everyone you know has your best interest at heart. People have an opinion on everything. They may not understand you. Some will do everything in their power to put you down, but you can't allow them. Again, God has given you the power to dominate your environment. Rebuke whatever unsettling things people say to you and stick to what God has put on your heart and in your mind.

Say this prayer with me:

I declare and decree that every vision and dream that You have shown me about my life and my family life will come to pass. I cancel any backlash and retaliation of my life and anything that I've shared that the enemy wants to destroy. I declare and decree that I will seek Your face through all challenges and trust in You to lead the way for me. I will accomplish the goals that I have written, and I won't let people's opinions dictate my future. In Jesus Name I pray, Amen.

G) Do it afraid. The Lord will make provision- There are so many things that the Lord has called us to. Sometimes we don't know where or how to begin. There are visions and dreams that you have seen yourself in, but there are times when it seems like it's not within our grasp. You may feel incapable, unworthy, unqualified, and afraid. The best thing to do is strategically ask the Lord for guidance because He will make provisions. For example, I have wanted to write a book for so long but I was worried I wasn't well established or had everything together but that was not the case for me. I still knew what I wanted to write but didn't know how I was going to do it. But let me tell you, once I wrote the outline and prayed to ask God for guidance, the words started to come out and I began to write. Despite doubt and worry, here I am completing this book to hopefully make an impact in someone's life. I still have a lot of work to be done.

Say this prayer with me:

Dear Lord, I know that at times I can be in my head and doubt myself and my capabilities. I want to be able to go when You tell me to go without opposition or confusion. Help me to trust You and believe that You will make provision in any and every area of my life. Give me the ability to trust and believe in myself and my abilities. I come before You with a heart that desires to do good despite fear. Grant me courage and strength to face uncertainties, knowing that You are with me. Help me overcome any apprehensions that may hinder me from spreading kindness and making a positive impact.

May Your love empower me to step out on faith, trusting that Your guidance will lead me on the path of goodness. Let me be a vessel of Your light, dispelling darkness through acts of compassion and love. Give me the confidence to do good, even when fear attempts to hold me back. I pray for courage, resilience, and a heart filled with Your love. In Jesus name I Pray, Amen.

CHAPTER 23

EMBRACING GOD'S WORK IN MY LIFE

I've read through the book and reflected on myself. It's a mirror reflecting some parts of life through writing. I read through the examples of the faith I had in every situation. I was facing a situation that I lost all hope in, but when I read through the chapters, I was inspired by how God moved in my life and how He is still moving. I had to reclaim hope, and trust that God was my source of joy, peace, and deliverance. I had to repossess what the enemy had taken from me. I want to say that the struggles and circumstances we face are not a form of punishment from God or a result of something we did wrong. But the thing is, there are certain obstacles you must go through to be pruned and sharpened in a certain area. As we face these challenges, remember these experiences are to equip us for the promise that God has set forth for us and our God-given destiny.

We are all called to a certain audience, and certain people that might share our testimony. They are the ones that will help us thrive. For instance, it's hard to help someone if you've never been in or faced their situation. Challenges and struggles in life serve as God's way of testing and refining us spiritually and in our prayer life. Take me, for example; I considered myself a decent Christian, attended church regularly, read my Bible habitually, and Would pray 1 while going through the motions of life, but I never truly had a deep relationship with God. What led to a deeper relationship with God was a prolonged season where I felt cornered, forced to engage in spiritual warfare, and to utilize all available resources to navigate and resolve the situation. But at the end of the day, God is the one who moved. He's the one who got the final say, because when I look at myself now, compared to back then, I'm so much stronger spiritually, than I've ever been in my life. Even when things go wrong, I don't falter. Granted I get sad with some disappointments, but I don't stay there. After moving forward, I realize that God is not only my Redeemer but also my Restorer. Nothing is impossible for Him; I've witnessed His intervention in my life during challenging situations, not only for me, but for my family and friends. There have been situations that surprised me, instances where I doubted, which is normal, but God reminded me of my prayer closet. He recalled those moments when I prayed with tears streaming down my face, realizing that He truly heard me. Sometimes, we pray for immediate action, but it's crucial to understand that God hears our pleas and cries. He moves at the right time, ensuring His glory is revealed. We must lean on Him, especially in a world that's not improving or looking to Him.

We must grow stronger, standing firm on the Word of God as our support in challenging situations and avoiding the temptation to give up. Instead of saying, "I can't take this anymore," we need to say "God, I trust You" or "I leave this in Your capable hands" and believe it. While others may empathize with our struggles, only God truly comprehends our secret tears, the depths of our emotions, and the effort it takes to present ourselves. He alone sees every aspect of our lives, making Him the only one we should place our hope and trust. Because Hope Is Here!

REFLECTIVE QUESTIONS

How has your belief in being an overcomer and conqueror shaped your perspective during difficult times?

_____

_____

_____

_____

In what ways has holding yourself accountable impacted your personal growth and relationships?

_____

_____

_____

_____

Reflecting on the power of prayer and unstoppable faith, how have these principles strengthened your spiritual journey?

_____

_____

_____

_____

How do you maintain perseverance and push forward, even when faced with opposition or challenges?

_____

_____

_____

_____

BIBLE VERSES

Isaiah 40:31 *"But those who hope in the Lord will renew their strength. They will soar on wings like eagles; they will run and not grow weary, they will walk and not be faint."*

Psalm 34:17-18 *"The righteous cry out, and the Lord hears them; He delivers them from all their troubles. The Lord is close to the brokenhearted and saves those who are crushed in spirit."*

CLOSING PRAYER:

Heavenly Father, I come before You with a heart full of gratitude and humility, reflecting on Your promises in Isaiah 40:31 and Psalm 34:17-18. Lord, I thank You that when I place my hope in You, You renew my strength. In times when I feel weak or weary, You lift me up, giving me the ability to soar on wings like eagles. When the road ahead feels long and difficult, You empower me to run without growing tired, to walk without becoming faint. You are the source of my endurance, my strength, and my hope.

Father, I also reflect on the beauty of Your promise in Psalm 34. You hear the cries of the righteous, and You are near to the brokenhearted. I thank You that in my moments of pain, when my spirit feels crushed by the weight of my burdens, You do not turn away. Instead, You draw closer, bringing comfort, peace, and deliverance. Lord, I ask that You remind me of Your presence when I feel alone and help me to trust that You see my pain and are working to bring healing.

For those moments when my heart is heavy and the trials seem overwhelming, I pray that You continue to be my refuge and strength. When life feels uncertain, remind me that You are the God who sustains, the One who restores and renews. Help me to be patient and trust in You as I wait, knowing that You are faithful to deliver me from all my troubles.

Lord, as I walk through life's challenges, may I never forget that Your strength is made perfect in my weakness. Let me lean into You, relying not on my own abilities but on Your grace and power. And in the moments when I stumble, may I find comfort in Your nearness, trusting that You will always lift me up again. Thank You, Father, for being my source of hope, for hearing my cries, and for being close to my broken heart.

In Jesus' name I pray, Amen.

I END WITH THIS:

No matter how much you care for someone; you can't make the decision for them to change their life or lifestyle on your own. Only the authority of God and the person's willing heart and mind can cause a real transformation. You can plead and beg and threaten but nothing will genuinely change until God steps in and gives that person a change of heart. God has given you a voice to speak, to dominate and to change your environment (Genesis 1:26). Make all your requests known to Him about your loved ones and wait (Psalms 47:9). But don't be dormant, be active in the assignment(s) that God has for you. When you focus on Him alone, He will make things clear and light. So, be patient, everything that you have been waiting for will be yours. God wants you to heal and be the best version of yourself. He wants you to let go. It's not too late for you no matter what you think, feel, or see. Let Him in and allow Him to do the work in you. He didn't give you those dreams and aspirations to stay stagnant. Write your visions and make them plain. It's your season to shine. There is nothing too small or too big for God to do in your life.

> **Matthew 11:29** *"Take My yoke upon you and learn from Me, for I am gentle and humble in heart, and you will find rest for your souls."*

I would like to hear about your testimony and journey with this book. You can contact me through:

Email: Olindagiveshope@gmail.com
Facebook: Olinda Gacin-Desrosiers
Instagram: @olindagiveshope

I look forward to hearing from you!

LETTER TO HUBBY

Dear Geno a.k.a My Love,

As I reflect on the journey of our life together—17 years as a couple and 15 years as husband and wife—all I can say is, "But God." Sometimes I pinch myself, wondering if this is real, like a beautiful melody "I Gotta Be" from Jagged Edge. This journey with you has been nothing short of incredible.

From the start, we were young and a little naïve, navigating marriage without a blueprint. Neither of us was taught how to be a spouse; we acted more on emotions and feelings than on faith. But God stepped in. He interrupted our plans and allowed us to grow—individually and as a couple. Through it all, He made us stronger. He turned our trials into testimony, enabling us to bless others—friends, family, and couples—who are facing their own challenges.

Though we haven't mastered marriage (and never will), we learn and grow every day. I thank God for what we've endured because He knew we could handle it. His word reminds us that He never gives us more than we can bear, and we've overcome so much together. Those hardships have become stepping stones, allowing us to share wisdom and strength with others.

I won't lie—this journey has been hard. There were times I questioned God, times I wanted to leave, and times you did too. But God always had the final say. Even when I tried to take my own path, He lovingly redirected me. Through random people, divine moments, and His still, small voice, He reminded me to stay the course.

I'm grateful for the strength to listen, to stay committed, and to trust God's plan. The transformation I've seen in us—individually and as a couple—has been nothing short of miraculous. Stepping out of His way and letting Him move has brought joy and peace beyond anything I could have imagined.

Today, I smile every time I hear your voice, every time I see your face. I thank God for the man you've become, the father you are to our children, and the spiritual covering you provide for our family. You lift me up when I feel weak, guide me when I stray, and love me through my strong-willed nature. Your patience with me has been a gift, and I thank God for giving you the grace to love and understand me as I am.

Because of God's love, I've been able to love you more deeply, beyond the challenges we've faced. Together, we've built a beautiful family and a bond that continues to grow stronger every day. I thank God for your life, and I am excited to see where this journey takes us next. Sharing our story with the world is just the beginning, and I know He has great plans for us.

I love you with all my heart and look forward to continuing this amazing journey with you, hand in hand.

Forever yours,

Cherie

REFERENCES

God, The Father, The Son, and the Holy Ghost

Oates, J. (16 January 2022). Christian Disciplines. Types of Christian Fasting & Whats Right for You. https://justdisciple.com/fasting-types/https://justdisciple.com/fasting-types/

Fasting. (2022). Retrieved January 17, 2022, from https://en.wikipedia.org/wiki/Fasting

Christian Disciplines Julia Oates. Retrieved January 22, 2022, https://justdisciple.com/fasting-types/

NOTES

NOTES

NOTES

NOTES